Messiah in Weakness

Messiah in Weakness

A Portrait of Jesus from the
Perspective of the Dispossessed

Yung Suk Kim

CASCADE *Books* • Eugene, Oregon

MESSIAH IN WEAKNESS
A Portrait of Jesus from the Perspective of the Dispossessed

Copyright © 2016 Yung Suk Kim. All rights reserved. Except for brief quotations in critical publications or reviews, no part of this book may be reproduced in any manner without prior written permission from the publisher. Write: Permissions, Wipf and Stock Publishers, 199 W. 8th Ave., Suite 3, Eugene, OR 97401.

Cascade Books
An Imprint of Wipf and Stock Publishers
199 W. 8th Ave., Suite 3
Eugene, OR 97401

www.wipfandstock.com

PAPERBACK ISBN: 978-1-4982-1745-3
HARDCOVER ISBN: 978-1-4982-1747-7
EBOOK ISBN: 978-1-4982-1746-0

Cataloguing-in-Publication data:

Names: Kim, Yung Suk.

Title: Messiah in weakness : a portrait of Jesus from the perspective of the dispossessed / Yung Suk Kim.

Description: Eugene, OR: Cascade Books, 2016 | Includes bibliographical references and index.

Identifiers: ISBN 978-1-4982-1745-3 (paperback) | ISBN 978-1-4982-1747-7 (hardcover) | ISBN 978-1-4982-1746-0 (ebook)

Subjects: LCSH: Asthenia—Biblical teaching | Jesus Christ

Classification: BT301.2 K52 2016 (print) | BT301.2 (ebook)

Manufactured in the U.S.A.   MAY 23, 2016

This book is dedicated to the memories
of my mother In-Soon Kim with love

Table of Contents

Acknowledgments ix

Chapter 1: Introduction 1
   Jesus and Weakness 4
   Portrayals of Jesus 6
   An Alternative View of Jesus: "Messiah in Weakness" 16
   Chapter Outline 22

Chapter 2: The View of Weakness in the Hellenistic-Roman World 24
   Political Ideology in the Roman Empire 24
   Hellenistic Schools of Thought and View of Weakness 27
   Summary 33

Chapter 3: The View of Weakness in Jewish Tradition 35
   View of Weakness in the Creation Story 35
   Deuteronomistic Works 38
   Prophetic Writings 39
   First-Century Judaism 42
   Jesus' View of Weakness 43
   Summary 46

Chapter 4: Jesus' Experience and Interpretation of Weakness 47
   Jesus' Experience of Weakness 49
   Jesus' Interpretation of Weakness 53
   Summary 68

Chapter 5: Jesus' Enactment of Weakness 69
   Teaching in Parables 70

Social Activism 95
Healing and Exorcism 97
Summary 105

Chapter 6: Jesus' Crucifixion as a Paradox of Weakness 106
Jesus' Crucifixion as a Paradox of Weakness 107
Jesus' Crucifixion as out of Weakness 107
Jesus' Crucifixion as Holy Death of Love 109
Jesus' Crucifixion as Weakness that Demands Justice 115
Summary 117

Chapter 7: Conclusion 119
Laozi's *Tao Te Ching* and Weakness 121
Weakness as a New Paradigm for Humanity 124
Excursus: Reading Biblical Characters through the Eyes of Weakness 126

Bibliography 135
Subject Index 143

Acknowledgments

I AM VERY PLEASED to dedicate this book to the memories of my mother In-Soon Kim with love. She may have been weak as a woman, but very strong as a mother. I grew up seeing how much she gave up for her children and how strong she was through her life of weakness. She taught me what it means to live in weakness—not by word, but through tears and sweat. So I dedicate this book to honor my mother's life. I also would like to give my special thanks to Larry Welborn, Professor of New Testament at Fordham University. No word of mine can be adequate enough to express my deepest gratitude for his presence in my work. I also want to express my sincere thanks to Mitzi Smith, Associate Professor of New Testament at Ashland Theological Seminary, who has been supportive of my research. More than anything, she is a true inspiration to my ongoing work. I also thank my teachers at Vanderbilt University. Among others, Daniel Patte, Professor of New Testament emeritus, and Fernando Segovia, Oberlin Graduate Professor of New Testament and Early Christianity, have nurtured me as a scholar, strengthening my academic skills and lenses in biblical studies. I also like to express my heart-felt thanks to Dean Kinney, faculty, staff and students at the School of Theology at Virginia Union University for their unwavering support of me as a beloved member of the community. I thank all of my students for sharing their struggles and stories with me.

Above all, nothing would have been possible without my family's love and support. My wife YongJeong's sacrifice and love for the family are beyond comparison. I give a big round of hugs to my daughters, HyeRim, HyeKyung, and HyeIn. Particular thanks to HyeIn, who read the entire manuscript and gave me a fresh, loving response.

1

Introduction

MODERN CULTURE AND PHILOSOPHY are built on a long-standing, reason-based positivism about the human condition. Socrates in the West believed in the power of true knowledge, and Laozi in the East also had confidence in the power of nature through which people can live a just, peaceful life. Modernity, by and large, is a direct heir of the Western civilization in which liberty and individualism are among the most important driving forces in people's lives. Overall, the human condition has been greatly improved because of this "reasonable" approach to the world and religion. Today epidemics are treated from medical and scientific perspectives, not from spiritual or magical perspectives. Viruses are identified and tackled.

In modern days, people tend to believe that personal and social maladies can be dealt with with medical techniques that remove or combat harmful invaders. The idea is that health or strength can be maintained by removing the source/phenomenon of weakness, whether physical, spiritual, personal, or communal. Similarly, the young are advised to "be strong and do not show your emotions or tears even when things get rough because they are signs of weakness." In a way, people are brainwashed to believe that strength/power is the opposite of weakness. However, the problem is that there is not much discussion about what constitutes strength or what it means to be strong. In the dominant modern view, strength/power comes from a mastery of knowledge, confidence about the self, strong will to carry out plans, and/or virtues such as self-control. But I would like to suggest strength/power can be understood differently; it can also come through the experience of weakness in our lives or in the world. Whereas the dominant concept of power has to do with changing or controlling others or things, the alternative concept has more to do with empowering others through empathy.

This alternative understanding of strength/power may seem strange to Christians who believe that humans are supposed to be strong and that human or social weakness is the result of sin. Likewise, all forms of weakness are simply seen as negative or useless personal, moral deficiencies, or physical, spiritual frailties, or adverse conditions of the social environment. They hardly accept their aging or dying, aspiring to live forever with an extension of this bodily life. Indeed, a literal reading of the Genesis creation story conveys an impression that if Adam and Eve had not sinned in the Garden of Eden, they and their descendants (all human families) would have lived forever without tasting death. But the creation story describes the difficult human conditions that people had to deal with in ancient times.[1] So much so that it is not an accident that the Apostles' Creed writes a belief in the bodily resurrection: ". . . believing in the resurrection of the body." But this idea of the resurrection of the body is not Jesus' idea or the mainline Jewish idea. Jesus clearly rejects bodily resurrection when asked by the Sadducees: "In the resurrection, then, whose wife of the seven will she be? For all of them had married her" (Matt 22:28). Jesus answers them: "You are wrong, because you know neither the scriptures nor the power of God. For in the resurrection they neither marry nor are given in marriage, but are like angels in heaven. And as for the resurrection of the dead, have you not read what was said to you by God, 'I am the God of Abraham, the God of Isaac, and the God of Jacob'? He is God not of the dead, but of the living'" (Matt 22:29–32). Here Jesus' point is that God is in the present through people's lives. The continuous presence of God is more important than any other claims about God. Yes, Jesus believes in resurrection, but that is not of the bodily in nature. So the right biblical phrase about resurrection must be "the resurrection of *the dead*," not the body.

Paul also says that resurrection is not about the bodily in nature, but is to be understood spiritually. He also uses the phrase "the resurrection of the dead," not the body (1 Cor 15:12). If the resurrection body is a body at all, Paul understands that it is a kind of "spiritual body" (1 Cor 15:44). This phrase "the spiritual body" is oxymoronic according to Greek philosophy in which the body cannot go hand in hand with the spirit. Paul's point is that God has power and will prevail in the end. People will be hopeful because of that. God will make the dead live. Paul's resurrection language

---

1. Meyers, *Discovering Eve*, 47–71.

assures Christians about their lives through faith. Otherwise, resurrection is not an extension of this bodily life, as Paul writes: "flesh and blood cannot inherit the kingdom of God" (1 Cor 15:50).

In the traditional view of power/strength, people believe that the only way to get out of this "fatal" weakness embedded in humanity and the world is to believe in Jesus who took the form of weakness for them and died on the cross *in weakness*.[2] Here the claim is that Jesus came down from heaven—a place of all power and strength, and chose a life of weakness even though he was not weak and died for humanity voluntarily. God became human to save humanity from their weakness once and for all. Through this "strong" Jesus, Christians will be ultimately free from all forms of weakness—suffering, sorrow, sickness, and death.[3]

However, this one-sided dominant view of humanity fails to address the complexities of weakness, which are part of human condition and human transformation.[4] Weakness is broadly defined not only as personal/social conditions but as a virtue that refers to mercy, solidarity, and change of mind.[5] At any rate, we cannot deny that weakness is part of the human condition, and we have to ask why there is weakness in our lives, society, and the world at large. Some weakness is embedded in humanity. We are all vulnerable to disasters, natural or human-made. Other forms of weakness are human-made; some people live in poverty, for instance, because of the rich's exploitation. Given the various forms of weakness the desired response is an act of mercy toward the weak.

---

2. Later we will investigate 2 Cor 13:4 in which "in weakness" is one possible translation of *ex astheneias*. But this Greek phrase has a plain sense of "out of, by, because of." A more plausible translation of 2 Cor 13:4 would be: "he (Jesus) was crucified by weakness, but lives by the power of God." Then, why the majority of the English Bibles including the NRSV and NIV have "in weakness" instead of "by or out of" seems clear that they want to make sure about Jesus' vicarious voluntary salvific death. We will come back to this issue later.

3. A strong belief in the complete freedom from all weakness in the end is not only apocalyptic but also dualistic in the sense that the ultimate salvation is not in this world but in heaven—an influence of Neo-Platonism in the third century CE.

4. This book's basic assumption about humainty is as follows: "Weakness is part of human condition and transformation." Namely, humans are supposed to live with weakness. More than that, because of weakness, they can be transformed. Later in this chapter we will see more about the relation between weakness and transformation by exploring "the eyes of weakness."

5. For the importance of weakness as vulnerability and openness to others, see Hauerwas, *Living Gently*.

Jesus and Weakness

To some people Jesus becomes a hindrance to God's revelation because they see only Jesus without looking at God to whom Jesus points his finger. Jesus does not preach about himself but proclaims "the good news of God" (*euangelion tou theou*) (Mark 1:14).[6] Jesus does not say believe in me but "believe in the good news (of God)" (Mark 1:15).[7] The good news is not about Jesus but about God. Jesus is not the primary source of good news. Rather, he testifies to the truth of God, as indicated in John 18:37, and embodies the good news of God through his costly journey of faith. Therefore, if we do not distinguish between God and Jesus, Jesus becomes an idol that keeps us from seeing who God is or what God requires us to do. Micah seems to deliver a good word about that: "O mortal, what is good; and what does the LORD require of you but to do justice, and to love kindness, and to walk humbly with your God?" (Micah 6:8).

In this idolatrous view of Jesus, his crucifixion is understood merely as salvific atonement through which sins are dealt with and cleansed.[8] But in fact, Jesus' death would be unthinkable if he did not proclaim the good news of God in a hostile world. His lifelong ministry and message is focused on God's good news and his rule: "The time is fulfilled and God's rule has come near; change your mind and believe in the good news" (Mark 1:15). Jesus was willing to die for God's good news and God's rule in the here and now. But this does not mean that his death is necessary or that his suffering is good. Jesus' mission is not to die for humanity as a sin offering but to proclaim God's rule on earth.

As we see above, the historical Jesus has been understood in ways that remove him from the very struggle he had in proclaiming God's good news.[9] The popular view of Jesus is that Jesus is strong and divine from his

---

6. The genitive phrase "the good news of God" is rendered with the subjective genitive meaning that God is good news. For example, God is good news because of his character or action expressed with mercy, love, and justice. The genitive phrase can be also rendered an objective genitive, which means the good news about God or good news from God. In all of these, the bottom line is that the good news of God is not about Jesus. Jesus is the one who proclaims about God. See Kim, *Resurrecting Jesus*, 48–73.

7. Ibid., 53–66.

8. Martyrdom theology is reflected in later epistles of the New Testament (Deutero-Pauline and Pastoral Letters and Hebrews) and other early Christian writings such as the Martyrdom of Polycarp (156 CE). In later Christian times suffering for others is understood as a characteristic of the apostle (Col 1:23–24).

9. Scholars do not have consensus about who the historical Jesus was. But I argue

birth to death, and therefore that he only identifies with the weak. In other words, Jesus himself was not weak.[10] This view explains away the weakness of Jesus that results in his crucifixion. However, Paul so clearly states that "Jesus was crucified *out of weakness (ex astheneias)*" (2 Cor 13:4a). Paul does not hide the fact that Jesus was crucified because of weakness. *Ex astheneias* means "out of weakness," "by weakness," or "because of weakness." I wonder why then the NIV and others including the NRSV translate *ex astheneias* as "in weakness," as if Jesus suffered voluntarily. In my judgment, translators or editors of those English Bibles have interest in making sure that Jesus' crucifixion is voluntary and salvific. But there are two problems with this kind of translation. On the one hand, the problem is that evil hands behind Jesus' crucifixion are not questioned or named. Even though Jesus risks his life for God's good news, his tragic death is not the goal of his life; it is the consequence or price of his work. On the other hand, the problem is that questions about theodicy are not raised, as if God allowed Jesus to be crucified for salvation of humans. Actually, Jesus' death is tragic and it is not wanted by God or Jesus. If Jesus' message about God's rule had been accepted by people, he would not have been crucified. In Paul's view Jesus was a weak human being like any other. That is to say, Jesus could not avoid his tragic death as long as he continued proclaiming God's rule on earth.

Paul does not stop at Jesus' crucifixion by weakness. He goes on to declare God's power: "but [Jesus] lives by the power of God" (2 Cor 13:4b). Jesus' crucifixion happened in the past, but now God makes him live now. Paul makes a distinction between Jesus and God. On the one hand, Jesus did his best and yet was crucified because of weakness. In other words, Jesus could not raise himself. His best job was to live for God even at the risk of his life. The next part is God's business. God vindicates Jesus by his power. In this way, Paul contrasts Jesus' weakness with God's power and in doing so he makes a distinction between God and Jesus. So the whole

---

that, as I did in my book *Resurrecting Jesus*, the historical Jesus is somewhat different from the portrayal of the New Testament. See Kim, *Resurrecting Jesus*, 29–31. In this book I listed four views of scholarship about the historical Jesus' relation to the New Testament. For more about a diversity of the historical Jesus studies, see Beilby, *The Historical Jesus*. See also Gowler, *The Historical Jesus;* Kee, *What Can We Know about Jesus?*; Powell, *Jesus as a Figure in History*.

10. In this view, Jesus "displayed God's love by dying for the 'weak'—the ungodly, the sinner, the enemy (Rom 5:6–10)." Gorman, *The Death of the Messiah*, 109. Similarly, Gorman says: "God is revealed as the one who operates through and among the weak— the weakness of the Messiah's shameful death on a Roman cross, which is indeed the weakness of God'" (109).

verse of 2 Cor 13:4 makes better sense if we translate it like this: "For he was crucified by weakness, but lives by the power of God." Here "by weakness" has a direct parallel with "by the power of God." But most English Bibles do not have this distinction or contrast between Jesus and God. By translating *ex astheneias* as "in weakness" they support the view of Jesus' salvific suffering or the redemptive suffering of God with Jesus.[11] In doing so, what is sacrificed is the negligence of evil power and complex meaning of his life and death. We will discuss more about Jesus' crucifixion and weakness in chapter 6.

Going against the above traditional approach to Jesus, this book examines Jesus' experience and understanding of weakness, broadly defined as all aspects of weakness that permeate every sphere of human life. For example, we can think of physical or spiritual frailty, intellectual limitedness, and adverse human conditions due to social ills or natural disasters. But more than that, weakness also can be understood as virtue opposed to the culture and philosophy in Jesus' time. The alternative wisdom and power is well summarized by Paul: "God's foolishness is wiser than human wisdom, and God's weakness is stronger than human strength" (1 Cor 1:25). The whole point is how we understand God's weakness or God's foolishness. Even though Jesus did not employ those terms that Paul used, he taught and lived with an alternative wisdom of God. For example, he taught that true life is to lose it (Mark 8:35–37; Matt 10:39; 16:25; Luke 9:24–5).

Portrayals of Jesus

As I briefly mentioned previously, Jesus scholarship has not paid much attention to a "weak" Jesus, who experiences weakness in himself and the world. So it is necessary to review the current landscape of historical Jesus studies, and I will limit discussion to a few major portrayals of the historical Jesus: the "Western" Savior Jesus, the apocalyptic prophet, Jesus the Liberator, and the Spirit-filled Reformer. After this, I will explore an alternative

---

11. This view of Jesus and his crucifixion is widely accepted by many scholars. Tomlin, *Power of the Cross*, 100, 278. See also Schlatter, *History of the Christ*, 287, 292–93; *Theology of the Apostles*, 188; idem, *Paulus, der Bote Jesus*, 669; Stott, *Cross of Christ*, 283; Ridderbos, *Paul*, 206–14; Gaffin, *Resurrection and Redemption*, 44–52. Stein, *Method and Message*, 19–20. France, *Jesus and the Old Testament*, 79–80, 106, 109, 117; Wenham, *Christ and the Bible*, 60; Barnett, *Message of 2 Corinthians*, 179. See also Calvin, *Institutes*, 2.2.10–11; Grabe, *Power of God*, 144–49. O'Collins, "Power Made Perfect in Weakness," 531, 536.

approach to the historical Jesus through "the eyes of weakness," which will be explored later in this chapter. With this new approach, one important question throughout is: How does Jesus interpret or respond to his experience of weakness and enact it through his life?

The "Western" Jesus the Savior

The "Western" Jesus the Savior is a dominant view of Jesus throughout history. That is to say, Jesus is not weak at all; he is both a perfect human being and divine.[12] In this view there is no real difference between the historical Jesus and the Jesus portrayed in the New Testament.[13] Jesus came to the world to save people from their sins through his death.[14] Dane Ortlund's statement summarizes this view well:

> Rather we are bringing out the way in which Jesus experienced what all our moral weakness deserved so that we can experience the strength of a righteous status before God simply by acknowledging that weakness, fleeing to Christ, and refusing to self-resource qualification before him. Because of Christ's vicarious weakness, divine power is channelled in admitting, not circumventing, our weakness.[15]

In this view, Jesus' humanity, by and large, disappears because everything Jesus does reflects his perfect power and love for the world. All his powerful works and even his death on the cross are possible because he is strong and divine, unlike other human beings. So they say that Jesus was crucified "in weakness" out of his love for humanity, as we have seen before in matters of translation. Jesus' vicarious death or weakness intends to save people from their weakness, as Ortlund observes: "Christ's vicarious weakness rescues weak people (cf. Rom 5:6). He became weak, bearing the wrath we deserved, so that our natural weaknesses might not dictate our usefulness in the kingdom, and, even more fundamentally, so that our

---

12. For example, see Bauckham, *Jesus and the God of Israel*, 32.
13. Johnson, *Real Jesus*; Wright, *Jesus and the Victory of God*. About full-fledged scholarship in fundamentalism, see Stein, *Jesus the Messiah*.
14. See Schlatter, *History of the Christ*, 204. Chapman, *Perceptions of Crucifixion*, 252–54. Gorman, *Inhabiting the Cruciform God*, 25–34, 121–23.
15. Ortlund, "Perfect in Weakness," 106.

moral weakness, once confessed, might not dictate our existence in the kingdom."[16]

Accordingly, in this view of the Jesus the Savior, weakness, whether personal or societal, is considered a result of Adam's sin. Without sin, humans were supposed to be strong because they were created in that way. To resolve this issue of unnecessary weakness in our human lives, Jesus becomes a new Adam who bore all human weakness with himself and restores humanity back to the original human as in the Garden of Eden. This kind of typical, popular understanding about human salvation from weakness is widespread among Christians and in theological studies. Again, Ortlund typifies such a view of Jesus and human weakness:

> Stated in biblical-theological terms, we could say that humans were created "strong"—morally strong, uninhibited in communion with God. The plunge into sin in Genesis 3 introduced both natural weakness (aging, disease, laborious toil) and, more deeply, moral weakness (a propensity toward idolatry, self-reliance, and hard-heartedness). Yet the odd way out of that weakness is not self-resourced strength but acknowledged weakness, brought to Christ. Such acknowledgment, due to Christ's vicarious and canonically climactic weakness on the cross, clears the way for God's strength. And in the consummated new earth, we will, once again, be strong (cf. 1 Cor 15:53)—this time, though, without even the possibility of weakness.[17]

As we see above, Ortlund believes that people can be strong through "Christ's vicarious and canonically climactic weakness on the cross." As a result, he argues, "we will, once again, be strong . . . without even the possibility of weakness." This implies that human strength is possible through Christ once and for all. In this view Jesus resolved all human weakness and made people strong once again. This Western Jesus permeates even minority churches in the United States. In church programs and activities, study materials, worship rituals, liturgical objects, and on the beautiful stained glass, Jesus is drawn like a brown-haired, white man, who is at the same time all-powerful.

---

16. Ibid., 105.

17. Ibid., 107. This view of weakness is the basis of traditional theology. See McGrath, *Luther's Theology of the Cross*; Kolb and Arand, *Genius of Luther's Theology*, 146–48. See also Moltmann, *Theology of Hope*; Bauckham, *Theology of Jürgen Moltmann*, 29–46; Dawn, *Powers, Weakness, and the Tabernacling*, 35–71.

Jesus the Apocalyptic Prophet

A majority of scholars believe that the historical Jesus predicted the end of the world and God's radical judgment would come during his life.[18] Paula

18. It is very plausible that Jesus may have thought of himself as the one who could bring God's kingdom to the world through his work in his lifetime. This view is based on several clues in the gospels and first-century Judaism. First, Mark 9:1 ("Truly I tell you, there are some standing here who will not taste death until they see that the kingdom of God has come with power") is read as authentic to Jesus' saying. But in my view Mark 9:1 is Mark's redaction. Historians believe that the Markan community is apocalyptic in that Jesus is pictured as the apocalyptic prophet. In Mark 13:32, Jesus says he does not know the timetable about such a final event: "But about that day or hour no one knows, neither the angels in heaven, nor the Son, but only the Father" (also in Matt 24:36). Jesus even says he is not good: "Why do you call me good? No one is good but God alone" (Mark 10:18). With these references, it is inferred that Jesus is not interested in telling such a firm date of God's judgment and completion of God's rule. The second clue is the fact that apocalypticism is the dominant movement and worldview in Jesus' time. Because of this cultural atmosphere, it is justifiable to see Jesus as part of this same apocalyptic religious climate. It is very plausible that Jesus may have preached about the last judgment of God, but there is no guarantee that he really followed the popular apocalyptic preaching like other apocalypticists. Actually, from his concerns about the sick and the marginalized and his teachings about God's rule in the here and now, it appears he is more interested in the quality of God's rule that makes impact on people's lives in the present. In Luke 17:20–21, Jesus refutes the Pharisees' concerns about the visible, temporal, territorial manifestation of God's kingdom: "Once Jesus was asked by the Pharisees when the kingdom of God was coming, and he answered, 'The kingdom of God is not coming with things that can be observed; nor will they say, 'Look, here it is!' or 'There it is!' For, in fact, the kingdom of God is among you." I do not mean that Jesus did not think about the when of God's rule. Certainly, he thought about the final completion of God's rule in the future, as most Jews in this time did. But in my view, unlike other apocalyptic Jews or Pharisees who place their focus in the future delivery of God's kingdom (like the dawning of the Messianic Age), Jesus is more realistic and practical about the present in his proclamation of God's good news and God's rule. According to Jesus, God's rule must be manifested in the lives of everyday people. Third, Jesus was a follower of John the Baptist, who was an apocalyptic prophet. This idea is very plausible, but there are two issues. First, as I argued in my recent work *Resurrecting Jesus* (36–38), even John the Baptist is not simply interested in the future judgment of God but very concerned about a lack/absence of God's rule in society. So John may not be a straight apocalyptic prophet who emphasizes merely future judgment. In other words, he may be interested more in transformation of the world now than future judgment. Second, even if John the Baptist were an apocalyptic prophet, there is no guarantee that Jesus followed John's apocalyptic view. In many ways, Jesus differs from his teacher, as I notes above with regard to his present-focused teaching about God's rule. For information, I list here some of the scholarly works regarding this view of the apocalyptic prophet Jesus. Barrett, *Jesus and the Gospel Tradition*; Allison, *Jesus of Nazareth*; Ehrman, *Jesus*; Fredriksen, *Jesus of Nazareth*; Lüdemann, *The Great Deception*; Meier, *A Marginal Jew*, Vol. 1, 2, 3; Sanders, *Jesus and Judaism*.

Fredriksen, among others, well summarizes such a view:

> The Jesus encountered in the present reconstruction is a prophet who preached the coming apocalyptic Kingdom of God. His message coheres both with that of his predecessor and mentor, John the Baptist, and with that of the movement that sprang up in his name. This Jesus thus is *not* primarily a social reformer with a revolutionary message; nor is he a religious innovator radically redefining the traditional ideas and practices of his native religion. His urgent message had not the present so much as the near future in view.[19]

According to this view, Jesus must be an apocalyptic prophet who believes that God would radically intervene in the world and bring forth a new world of the messianic age. So scholars put Jesus' preaching and work in the context of Jewish apocalypticism in the first century CE where Jewish prophets such as John the Baptist issue prophetic warnings. Likewise, in this same apocalyptic fervor Jesus is understood as one of these prophets who claims that the end is near. According to Mark 1, after John was arrested, Jesus takes over his work and goes back to Galilee, calling his twelve disciples for a possible apocalyptic mission aimed at a recovery of Israel.[20] In this apocalyptic view, Jesus is understood as a doomsday preacher who is overly concerned with the end of the world or the delivery of Israel.

But in fact, Jesus also emphasizes the presence of God's rule in the here and now (Luke 17:21). So the difficulty is how to explain his focus on the present rule of God. Overall, it is more persuasive to say that Jesus' primary concern is the changes now in people's lives than that he is a futuristic prophet. In his initial sermon in Mark 1:15, Jesus shows an emphasis on God's rule; that is, he asks people to change their attitude toward others so that the weak people may be welcomed into God's rule. Indeed, in Mark 1:15, Jesus uses the perfect tense concerning God's time and God's rule. He does not say that the time (that is God's time) will come or that God's rule will come. Rather, he declares that such a time and rule of God have come. That is why Jesus asks for a change of mind (*metanoia*) after his declaration of God's rule. If God's rule is being realized now, even gradually, Jesus does not have to emphasize too much the future kingdom of God.

The other problem with this view of the apocalyptic prophet is as follows: "Jesus is confident about his ability to predict the end of the world and

---

19. Fredriksen, *Jesus of Nazareth*, 266.
20. See Freyne, *Jesus, a Jewish Galilean*, 60–149.

to carry out God's revelation during his life time." But Jesus says he does not know the day or the time of the end in Mark 13:32 (cf. Matt 24:36): "But about that day or hour no one knows, neither the angels in heaven, nor the Son, but only the Father." I think this statement by Jesus is authentic because, according to the criterion of embarrassment, it is embarrassing to the evangelists, because he is supposed to know everything. Mark or Matthew could have changed this embarrassing statement, but preserved it. But one thing that is clear is that both of them did not invent it. Why would they create such an embarrassment themselves if they did not receive such a tradition? So the best reasoning is that this statement must derive from the very tradition about the historical Jesus, whose candid position about the time is "I don't know." In the normative Jewish tradition, there is a clear boundary between God and humans. So Jesus must be keenly aware of his humanity that cannot encroach upon God's area. This view is supported in Mark 10:18 where Jesus rebukes someone who calls him "good teacher." So I am convinced that Jesus has more focus on God's presence in the world now than on the mere future kingdom of God. We see a glimpse of such a practical purpose of God's rule in the here and now in John 9 where Jesus' main concern is to restore the sight of a man born blind, whereas his disciples' concern is to judge that person by wanting to know whose sin causes him to be born blind.

Jesus the Liberator

Whereas the "Western" Jesus the Savior comes to the world to die and save individuals as we have seen before, Jesus the Liberator comes to the world primarily to advocate for the marginalized and oppressed.[21] Jesus brings a message of hope and justice for the poor and proclaims the good news about God's rule in the here and now.[22] For this mission of the social gospel, Jesus criticizes the abusive and oppressive powers. Various forms of liberation theology adopt this view of a liberating Jesus: forexample, Black Theology, Latin American liberation theology, Minjung theology in Korea, and *Dalit* theology in India.[23] Here Jesus is also seen as being strong and

21. For example, see Sobrino, *Jesus the Liberator*.
22. Keck, *Who is Jesus?* 80–85.
23. For black theology of liberation, see Cone, *A Black Theology of Liberation*. Regarding Latin American liberation theology, see Sobrino, *Jesus the Liberator*. For Minjung theology in Korea, see Kim and Kim, *Reading Minjung Theology*. Regarding dalit

powerful and identifies with the weak and the oppressed. The only difference it has with the Western Jesus the Savior is the focus of Jesus' ministry. While the Western Jesus focuses on individual souls' salvation, the Liberator Jesus saves the marginalized from oppression in an unjust society or empire.

This view of a liberating Jesus focuses on external change such as transforming others or evil systems. Otherwise, there is not much emphasis on all aspects of change in relation to self or human life, including a change in self-knowledge; a change or renewal of self-critical examination; a change of personal attitude toward others, community, or society; or different ways of experiencing of the self, especially in difficult times.[24]

In this portrayal of Jesus we may also include other scholarly works such as those of John D. Crossan, Robert Funk, and Richard Horsley.[25] For Crossan and Funk, Jesus is the wise sage who tries to transform the world through his teaching.[26] For Horsley, Jesus is a prophet of social change:

> The focal concern of the kingdom of God in Jesus' preaching and practice, however, is the liberation and welfare of the people. Jesus' understanding of the "kingdom of God" is similar in its broader perspective to the confident hopes expressed in then-contemporary Jewish apocalyptic literature. That is, he had utter confidence that God was restoring the life of the society, and that this would mean judgment for those who oppressed the people and vindication for those who faithfully adhered to God's will and responded to the kingdom. That is, God was imminently and presently effecting a historical transformation. In modern parlance that would be labelled a revolution.[27]

theology, see Clarke, *Dalit Theology*.

24. I am concerned about partial aspects of transformation in biblical interpretation. For example, on the one end of the spectrum, the tendency is to emphasize an individual salvation or a change of heart without communal or social transformation. On the other end of the spectrum, the tendency is the opposite. Social transformation is explored without personal transformation. These extremes need to be mediated, and we should find an alternative view of transformation that involves both personal and public aspects of change. The *Journal of Bible and Human Transformation* (JBHT) was created to address diverse aspects of human transformation.

25. Crossan, *The Jesus Controversy*; *The Birth of Christianity*. See also Funk, *Honest to Jesus*. Patterson suggests that "Jesus was a wisdom teacher, and that the early Jesus movement thought of itself as a kind of wisdom school." Patterson, *The Gospel of Thomas and Jesus*, 232.

26. Ibid.

27. Horsley, *Jesus and the Spiral of Violence*, 206; *Hearing the Whole Story*; *Whoever*

In the view of the Jesus the Liberator, Jesus appears to be strong as the Son of God and shows no weakness at all. Because he is powerful and strong, he identifies with the weak and shows strong solidarity with them. Otherwise, there is not much discussion about Jesus' weakness or his response to the weakness in the world.

The Spirit-Filled Reformer

The view of the Spirit-Filled Reformer is taken from the work of Marcus Borg who takes the significance of the historical, spiritual Jesus back to our day.[28] In his book *Jesus: A New Vision*,[29] Borg rejects the popular image of a divine Jesus who came to the world to die for the redemption of sinners and then ascended to the heaven. He also rejects another popular image of Jesus as the apocalyptic (eschatological) prophet, who mistakenly predicted the end of the world in his own time. Borg rejects the first popular image because it portrays Jesus through the lens of post-Easter Christians. Such a portrayal is distant from the historical Jesus' life and death. Similarly, he rejects the second image of the apocalyptic prophet because Jesus can be read as a reformer of Judaism. Borg comes with a new angle of the historical Jesus based on Jesus' critical spirituality in the charismatic stream of Judaism.[30]

To support his thesis about such a historical, spiritual Jesus, Borg works on two organizing principles: Spirit and culture. First, regarding the Spirit, he argues that the world of the Spirit is real and that Jesus had deep, intimate relationships with the Spirit. Likewise, Jesus stands in the ecstatic, mystical tradition of biblical and Jewish religion. Borg lists the examples of these traits demonstrated by Jesus' internal life: his prayer life, the visions

---

Hears You Hears Me; *Bandits, Prophets, and Messiahs*; *Archaeology, History, and Society in Galilee*; *Galilee: History, Politics, People*; *Sociology and the Jesus Movement*; *The Liberation of Christmas*.

28. Marcus Borg's most recent book *The Heart of Christianity* evinces his mature thought and conviction about his faith. See also *The Meaning of Jesus*; *Conflict, Holiness, and Politics*; *Jesus: A New Vision*; *Jesus in Contemporary Scholarship*; *Jesus: Uncovering the Life, Teachings, and Relevance of a Religious Revolutionary*; *Meeting Jesus Again for the First Time*.

29. Borg, *Jesus: A New Vision*.

30. Stevan Davies also has a similar view that he emphasizes the spirit-possessed Jesus. But the difference is that while Borg emphasizes a counter-cultural prophetic spirit, Davies focuses on Jesus' charismatic power of the Spirit. See Davies, *Jesus the Healer*, 104.

he experienced, and his sense of intimacy with God. All his life was full of ecstatic, mystical experiences with the Spirit. The evidence of Jesus' spiritual life is found in his exorcisms and healing.

Second, Borg relates this reality of the Spirit with culture. That is to say, a Spirit-filled person could not remove himself from the culture in which he lived. In the biblical tradition, Israel's story itself was the story of the interaction between the world of the Spirit and the world of ordinary experiences. Moses and the prophets were also Spirit-filled mediators. The biblical tradition of Spirit-filled mediators is very significant to understanding the historical Jesus. The reality of another world (the invisible world of the Spirit) was not unusual to the people of the ancient world, unlike modern people who disregard the reality of the invisible world simply because it seems to be unscientific, superstitious, or psychotic.

In his cultural study, Borg shows a contrast between the politics of holiness and compassion. While the former means a separation of the pure from the impure, the latter means the way of Jesus who challenges the status quo by compassion. More specifically, Jesus challenges holiness-ridden culture that does not embrace the weak and marginalized in society. What is challenged is the conventional wisdom of the divisive hierarchical social world based on family, wealth, and honor. The social world of first-century Palestine was under the pressure of Roman occupation and was operated by the politics of holiness, which separated the pure from the impure, and insiders from outsiders. But Jesus challenged with the politics of compassion this prevailing holiness-ridden culture and the conventional wisdom of that social world, which centers on "family, wealth, honor, and virtue, all shaped by a religious framework."[31] This self-driven culture was the focus of transformation. Jesus was filled with God's compassion to change his social world into a transforming community of compassion, filled with love, acceptance, and inclusiveness. With the above analysis of Jesus in the culture, what follows is a summary of Borg's Jesus:

1. Jesus is a sage who critiqued the conventional wisdom of the Jewish social world by asking his people to turn to God rather than to their religion of holiness politics. The Spirit-filled Jesus called his people to center themselves on God, and to change their hearts and minds so that they see things in a new way: the narrow way, the way of "dying to the self" in place of the broad way that seeks wealth, power, honor, and this-worldly securities.

---

31. Ibid., 81.

2. As revitalization movement founder, Jesus focuses on renewal of Israel rather than creating a new religion, in the midst of crisis in the Jewish social world: "the growing internal division within Jewish society and the deepening of the conflict with Rome."[32] Jesus' renewal movement is summarized by his "alternative community with an alternative consciousness" rooted in the Spirit.[33] His alternative consciousness is to reverse the dominant consciousness of conventional wisdom through his vision of transforming Israel. Jesus calls his people to change their consciousness of holiness politics. Borg states that the revitalization movement stayed in the frame of Judaism. He put this rightly: "Jesus remained deeply Jewish, even as he radicalized Judaism."[34]

3. As a prophet, Jesus similarly assumes the job of the traditional prophets who indict, threaten, and call to change. Borg points out that "the purpose of the prophets was not to reveal the future, but to change it."[35] The author also points out that Jesus was not really speaking about the final judgment or about the kingdom of God that would come very soon. But Jesus' concern was just to change the present lives of his people by speaking out prophetic utterances to bring about real change of heart to God-centered.

4. Finally, Borg pictured Jesus as challenge; Jesus risked his life and went to Jerusalem to issue the call to change, and "to make a final appeal" to his people at the center of their national and religious life.[36] He states that the death of Jesus would be the result of his sojourn in Jerusalem, not the purpose of his journey. Jesus was killed because he sought to transform his own culture, in the power of the Spirit.

In conclusion, Borg's Jesus seems to be a good alternative to understanding the historical Jesus because his approach is not only historically critical but transformational in that Jesus appears as a cultural critic and reformer. However, he, like others, does not deal with Jesus' humanity in view of his experience of weakness in the world. If Borg had a balance between the Spirit and the "weak" part of Jesus, the picture of Jesus would have been more realistic or appealing to us.

32. Ibid., 142.
33. Ibid.
34. Ibid., 141.
35. Ibid., 154.
36. Ibid., 172.

In the end, what is lacking in all the major views of the historical Jesus, as we have examined so far, is that there is no critical exploration of weakness that is part of the human condition and/or human transformation. Because of this deficiency, there is a need for an alternative approach to Jesus: "Messiah in weakness."

An Alternative View of Jesus: "Messiah in Weakness"[37]

The Eyes of Weakness

The alternative view of Jesus focuses on the weakness that surrounds Jesus and the world. Of course, weakness is addressed by other historical Jesus studies, but it is not expressly dealt with, as we have seen before. But what is at stake is not simply a lens of weakness but the kind of lens used. As we have seen before, the traditional lens of weakness is negative. In it, the goal of life is to escape weakness, be it personal or communal, by belief in a Jesus who defeated it by his death. So it is important to define what kind of lens is employed in my study. A particular lens of weakness employed in this book is called "the eyes of weakness," which is a reading lens through which we see the world and Jesus. In addition, it is my argument that Jesus also employs this lens of weakness. From the outset, it must be said that the eyes of weakness involve the following characteristics:

1. All beings and non-beings in the world are weak and exist in weakness. For example, there is no person who is not weak. Weakness is

---

37. Messiah means "the anointed one" in Hebrew. It is not a divine title. Jesus the Messiah means that Jesus worked for God as the anointed one like a prophet or king. We should not assume that Jesus is the Messiah prophesied by the prophets in the Hebrew Bible, as commonly misunderstood by Christians. For more about this, see Becker, *Messianic Expectation*, 14–79. Generally speaking, while pre-exilic writings focus on the restoration of monarchism, post-exilic writings have more focus on theocracy, a return to the rule of God. It is only in the second and first century BCE when Palestine came under the control of Syria and Rome we see the first emerging root of messianic expectations. In difficult times such as this, as conveyed in Daniel, book of the apocalypse, there are two important issues: theodicy (Where is the just God?) and need to comfort those who are unjustly persecuted under the foreign powers. Naturally, people need a future deliverer. There are different candidates for such a figure (the anointed one): warrior type of the messiah like King David, Priestly messiah (in the Qumran community), or eschatological judge type in Daniel or 1 Enoch. However, Jesus does not belong to any of these images of the messiah. In this book what I mean by Jesus the Messiah is based on his self-understanding that he is working for God as a human agent of God. The historical Jesus is not believed to have claimed that he is the only Messiah or divine.

embedded in humanity. We are born with weakness and live through it and die because of it. We are not supposed to live forever without being sick, aging, or dying. Even non-living beings such as rocks or trees are weak. Rocks can be cracked by water and storms can knock down trees. Weakness is part of the human condition and the world.

2. Because of the realization that all are weak, we can see others as part of us. They are reflected as familiar faces of weakness. Through the eyes of weakness, we see others, who are also weak. This reading lens of weakness is different from finding fault in others. The eyes of weakness provide us with a new sense of deep solidarity bounded by weakness. Usually, the lens of weakness is not wanted by people because they want to identify with the strong.

3. Weakness can become the condition for strength if it is rightly understood and practiced, that is through an attitude of mercy. An analogy of water is helpful here. Water is weak *and* strong. A usual public perception about water is that though it is weak or soft, it is strong. But actually, that logic is not very telling because the strength of water lies in its very weakness. Because water is soft and weak, it can be gathered together into one place like a dam. Gathered water is transformed into great power if the dam releases water at once. We can say it in this way: Because water is weak or soft, it is strong. In other words, water's softness or weakness is the condition for strength. Here the weakness of water is a metaphor that speaks about the importance of a soft mind that responds to the brokenness of others and the self included. It is also a mind of mercy that seeks restoration of a person. We can be strong when we realize that we are weak and small. In this regard, weakness is a virtue that we have to embrace in our lives. Through that virtue, we find the world and ourselves standing strong.

4. When we or others go through a harsh world that results in social ills and injustices, we cannot sit still or watch faces of weakness in the world. This is the weakness that we have to engage with, advocating for the weak people. This is a mode of radical action of solidarity for the weak empowered by weakness—a virtue of mercy.

The Eyes of Deconstruction

The eyes of weakness are a deconstructive lens through which we dismantle the language of unity, control, especially the imperial univocal one because it prevents us from seeing the truth in the world.[38] What should be deconstructed is the familiar reading lens that seeks power or greatness without engaging in the world of weakness. With this deconstructive lens we see the importance of smallness in ourselves and the world. Babies cannot become adults in one day and plants cannot grow to their full potential in one hour. We can serve others gladly and feel great when we truly acknowledge that we are small before God and the world.

This deconstructive lens is also worn by Jesus who surprises his audience by reversing their customary expectations about God's kingdom or God's rule.[39] Jesus' hearers think that God's kingdom belongs to the strong, but Jesus says it is for the weak and all in the community. Jesus asks his disciples to embrace the little child, an icon or symbol of weakness, to show that God's kingdom needs such a "small" person (Matt 18:4). In the parable of the Pharisee and Publican (Luke 18:4), Jesus reverses the societal expectations about who is justified before God. It is not the Pharisee but the tax collector who is declared justified before God. From the parable proper, it is inferred that the miserable tax collector shows his "utter" weakness before God; he knows he is wrong and unfaithful. All he needs is the mercy of God. Because he is weak and humble, he finds the grace of God. So the sinner is declared justified not because he did great things but because he humbled himself in need of mercy. He is ready to receive the grace of God through his broken spirit. In contrast, the Pharisee did great things from the eyes of power in the world because he fasted and gave alms. He feels that he is strong and blessed. So he seems to ignore the tax collector who is weak and despicable due to his tax work. What is lacking with the Pharisee is a mind of mercy toward this weak man.[40] He does not seem to know that

---

38. Derrida, *Of Grammatology*.

39. For example, Jesus says: "All who exalt themselves will be humbled, and all who humble themselves will be exalted" (Matt 23:12; cf. Luke 14:11). Not only Jesus but biblical teachings in general in the Hebrew Bible (or in Jewish tradition) teaches this paradoxical , deconstructive truth that the humble will be lifted up; for example: Prov 29:23; Ps 138:6. Sage Laozi in the East also teaches about this. For example, he says: "Loss is gain, and gain is loss" in chapter 42 of the *Tao Te Ching*. We will explore his thought and wisdom in the last chapter of this book.

40. Again, John 9 reminds us of the importance of lens that we employ. In it, Jesus' disciples are more interested in the cause of a man born blind than in the healing of that man. In contrast, Jesus sees the need of that blind man and heals him.

God loves this weak miserable man too. In the end the Pharisee is declared not to be justified before God. It is not because he did something wrong in his work but because he judged the tax-collector to be hopeless. Apparently, the Pharisee does not know that his righteous standing before God requires his extending mercy to the most undeserving, like a tax-collector, because he is also a member of God's house.

Interpreting Jesus through the Eyes of Weakness

It seems very plausible that Jesus sees the world through the eyes of weakness that we just explored. Jesus is dispossessed and goes through ups and downs in his life.[41] Yet he does not give in to the adverse social conditions and is led to the Spirit. He surrenders to God by being baptized at the Jordan and goes on his journey of faith to realize God's rule on earth. I think Jesus said something like this in his journey, as Paul said: "My grace is sufficient for you, for power is made perfect *in weakness* . . . for whenever I am weak, then I am strong" (2 Cor 12:9–10).[42]

For Jesus, humans' problems are not simply because they are weak but because they do not acknowledge their weakness before God and other

---

41. In next chapter we will explore Jesus' experience and interpretation of weakness as he is faced with so many personal and communal issues under the pressure of the Roman Empire.

42. Paul's view of weakness is often hotly debated. See Sumney, "Paul's 'Weakness,'" 71–91. See also Roetzel, "Language of War," 77–99; Shaw, "Body/Power/Identity," 269–312; Glancy, "Boasting of Beatings," 99–135. Paul's view of "weakness" plays an important role in his ministry and he defends his apostleship through the subversive rhetoric of weakness. 2 Corinthians is a test case for him to show such a strategy, as he heavily uses weakness-related words there: 2 Cor 10:10; 11:21b—12:13 (the Fool's Speech); 13:3, 4, 9. From this letter, we know that Paul acknowledges his weakness in many ways (his physical illness, dull speech, and etc), and Shaw rightly observes about this: Paul was of "shame, humiliation, degradation, and . . . that which was morally bad." See Shaw, "Body/Power/Identity," 303. Paul's opponents in Corinth say that he is unfit for ministry because of his weakness as described above. Yet Paul subverts the dominant discourse on the body and power, using his weakness as a tool of "resistance" (Shaw's opinion) and "negotiation" (Roetzel's view) toward his opponents such as the super-apostles. See Shaw, "Body/Power/Identity," 311–12; Roetzel, "Language of War," 97–98. Regarding the language of resistance, Welborn also argues convincingly that Paul plays the runaway fool, as he is dubbed a coward runaway from Damascus as described in 2 Cor 10:1–6. Paul contrasts him with the braggart warrior who ruins and controls the weak bodies. See Welborn, "Runaway Paul," 115–63. Welborn also demonstrates the importance of Paul's "fool" strategy to counter the ideology of the powerful in Corinth and elsewhere in bringing the power of God for the weak. See his other work such as *Paul, the Fool of Christ*.

people. In order to teach people that because God is merciful to them they must embrace each other in God's kingdom, Jesus tells parables and heals the sick. Jesus lives in weakness for the weak. He advocates for those who are lost like sheep without a shepherd and shows solidarity with them, putting his life in harm's way.

His bold proclamation about God's good news for the weak infuriates those at the top of the social ladder. The result is a tragedy that Jesus is crucified[43] by evil powers and *out of* weakness. Today, in most parts of the world, if somebody talks about a politically innocuous message, he or she will not be charged and put to death. No one, in the time of Jesus, would be put in jail and put to death on the cross unless such a person brought significant potential threats against the Roman Empire or against the status quo in Judea. Jesus' boundary-breaking teaching and acts, as shown in his eating with tax-collectors and sinners, received attention from Pilate and other Jewish leaders who were suspicious about his actions. As a result of his bold proclamation about God's rule, not Rome's rule, Jesus is surely condemned to death on the cross by the Roman governor, Pilate (during 26–36 CE), who was in charge of law and order in Jerusalem during the reign of Tiberius (14–37).[44]

Seen through the eyes of weakness, Jesus' crucifixion is a tragic event, which he could not avoid because he chose a life of testimony for God's good news (not Rome's good news) and God's rule (not Rome's rule) on earth.[45]

---

43. Indeed, crucifixion is a most horrible form of punishment in the Roman Empire, reserved for non-Roman citizens who challenged the imperial power or the status quo: for example, runaway slaves or insurrectionists.

44. Both Josephus (38–100 CE), a Jewish historian and a contemporary of Jesus in the first century CE and Tacitus (c. 56–118 CE), a Roman historian, mention in their writings that Jesus was crucified by Pontius Pilate, the Roman governor. Tacitus records the following about Nero and Christians in Rome: "Therefore, to squelch the rumor, Nero created scapegoats and subjected to the most refined tortures those whom the common people called "Christians," a group hated for their abominable crimes. *Their name comes from Christ, who, during the reign of Tiberius, had been executed by the procurator Pontius Pilate.* Suppressed for the moment, the deadly superstition broke out again, not only in Judea, the land which originated this evil, but also in the city of Rome, where all sorts of horrendous and shameful practices from every part of the world converge and are fervently cultivated (*Italics for emphasis*)." Tacitus, *Annals* 15.44. The translation comes from Meier, *Marginal Jew*, 1:89–90. Josephus also mentions Jesus' crucifixion by Pilate in *Antiquities* 18.3.3.

45. Dale Allison believes that Jesus' crucifixion was certainly tragic as all the passion narratives in the Gospels do not hide that fact. Also from the tradition that preserves the memories of Jesus, the sketch of Jesus' horrific death in the Gospels seems true. So

He did not make peace with the political, religious powers at that time. Yet his journey of testimony is a struggling one, as the Markan Jesus prays like a person of dereliction: "My God, My God, why have you forsaken me?" (Mark 15:34; cf. Matt 27:46). We should know that Jesus in Mark certainly struggles because of his weakness. He asks God if there is another way that he could testify for the truth without suffering or facing danger. Jesus prays to God: "Abba, Father, for you all things are possible; remove this cup from me; yet, now what I want, but what you want" (Mark 14:36). In the end, Jesus realizes that there is no other way that he has to continue to preach about God's rule, not Rome's, even if he could be killed because of that. So we can interpret Jesus' crucifixion as his "difficult" love for God at the risk of his life, out of weakness. On the other hand, Jesus' crucifixion certainly raises questions about theodicy: Why would a good God allow such a horrendous thing to happen to Jesus? Where is God in this very evil scene of an innocent man's killing? Paul does not answer why Jesus was sacrificed by political powers other than by weakness. However, he deals with this evil power by declaring that God's power makes Jesus live. This is the language of vindication. However, while this language of vindication by Paul may be considered the best for many theologians today, it should not explain away the ugly face of evil and the horrendous suffering done to Jesus.

This new alternative reading of the historical Jesus with a focus on diverse aspects of weakness has great implications for Jesus-followers today. First, we have to know what kind of world we live in and how weak we are. This is the first thing we must know and check. We are created or born

---

Allison's position about Jesus' death is an intermediate stance between John D. Crossan's "prophecy historicized" and Raymond Brown's "history remembered." For Allison, the tradition about Jesus' passion is, overall, trustworthy and yet it should be carefully examined due to the instability of the memories of Jesus' death. See Allison, *Constructing Jesus*, 424–25. See also his *Theological Jesus*, 45–46; 62–66. See Brown, *Death of the Messiah*. While Brown basically trusts the gospel traditions about Jesus' death as remembered dynamically if not harmoniously, Crossan refutes the details about Jesus' death narrated in the Gospels, as he says: "My proposal is that Jesus' first followers knew almost nothing whatsoever about the details of his crucifixion, death, or burial. What we have now in those detailed passion accounts is not history remembered but prophecy historicized. And it is necessary to be very clear on what I mean here by prophecy. I do not mean texts, events, or persons that predicted or foreshadowed the future, that projected themselves forward toward a distant fulfilment. I mean such units sought out backward, as it were, sought out after the events of Jesus' life were already known and his followers declared that texts from the Hebrew Scriptures had been written with him in mind. Prophecy, in this sense, is known after rather than before the fact." Crossan, *Jesus: A Revolutionary Biography*, 163.

with both strength and weakness. That is who we are. If somebody denies this fact, he or she is disillusioned. Second, because we are not perfect, we have to see others in the same light, showing sympathy and solidarity. Taking one step further, we can participate in others' weakness. Third, in this reality we also should know that there are a variety of weaknesses in human lives and the world. Some forms of weakness are inexplicable: natural disasters like earthquakes or tsunami, for instance. Other kinds are human-made and should be dealt with accordingly. Since the origin of weakness is different, the solution/response must also be different. The weakness due to natural disasters cannot be fixed because we cannot control them. The best thing we can do to be present with those who are affected. But the weakness caused by evil hands or unjust powers can be fixed if there is a change of mind for the involved people or powers. Fourth, in the case of human-made weakness, injustices and evil are to be named and judged. A cheap forgiveness without demanding justice is another form of injustice. Those who are responsible for Jesus' crucifixion are to be judged. We live not by Jesus' death, which should not have happened, but by his faith that leads him to death. Living by his faith means to participate in his life of weakness and strength.

Chapter Outline

In chapter 2 we will examine the view of weakness in the Roman world because Jesus lived under the influence of Roman culture and philosophy. Though it is difficult to say how much Jesus was influenced by that dominant Hellenistic Roman philosophy and culture, he must have been under substantial pressure from that culture. Moreover, his audience also lived under imperial control. Therefore it is worth surveying the cultural atmosphere and philosophical understandings about weakness. In chapter 3 we will look into the view of weakness in the Jewish tradition and culture so that we may see differences and similarities with Jesus. Jesus was Jewish and familiar with Jewish scriptures and traditions. Overall, we will see in what sense Jesus continues or discontinues Jewish tradition in terms of the view of weakness.

In chapter 4 we will explore Jesus' experience of weakness in his personal, familial, and societal context. We will locate the possible locations of his weakness. At the same time we will see how Jesus interprets (or responds to) his experience of weakness. Jesus as a person of "true weakness" is in close contact with the Spirit and challenges hardened hearts to be weak before God and the world. Jesus does not romanticize weakness merely as surrendering to God. Reinterpreting rituals and laws, what he wants to achieve is to be strong through weakness, which is a metaphor of mercy or flexible mind toward others. In chapter 5 we will see how Jesus enacts an alternative view of weakness and how fiercely he loves people and challenges those who are stiff-necked toward others. Jesus teaches in parables to let people know that everyone is worthy of God's mercy and love. At the same time he wants people to re-imagine God's rule that is full of mercy. He also heals the sick to restore them to the normalcy of their lives. In chapter 6 we will deal with Jesus' crucifixion in view of weakness. Jesus' death on the cross is a paradox that reveals both his ultimate weakness that demands the justice of God (theodicy), and his unyielding spirit of love for the world and truth of God. In the end, a new portrait of Jesus will emerge from the "weak" Jesus who himself is dispossessed and yet empowered "to testify to the truth" of God (John 18:37). This view of Jesus distinctly contrasts the hitherto widely accepted "strong" Jesus who merely identifies with the weak.

Chapter 7 concludes the book and brings Jesus' view of weakness into dialogue with Laozi's. In fact, the two of them are similar in their approach to human wisdom and ethics. We will look into Laozi's book, *Tao Te Ching* (Dao De Jing) to see his view of weakness and the world. Lastly, I have an excursus at the end of the book in which some important characters in the Hebrew Bible are read from the eyes of weakness.

2

The View of Weakness in the Hellenistic-Roman World

JESUS LIVED IN THE Hellenistic-Roman world where "weakness" was, directly or indirectly, discussed and dealt with. For example, the social norm and culture in Jesus' time teaches that women are weak and that they are subordinate to men. The ruling class and elite in the Roman world say that strength comes from knowledge, social status, and wealth. To support the hierarchical worldview of the Roman Empire, Stoicism teaches that order or unity in society is more important than human dignity or equality. Jesus lived under this particular culture and philosophy that we have to analyze. While it is difficult to judge how much Jesus was influenced by the culture and philosophies in the Roman-Hellenistic world, it is not difficult to say that he must have responded to that world and culture in one way or another. So it is necessary to examine the political ideology of the Empire and major philosophical systems, including Hellenistic Judaism. However, I do not attempt to fully cover all literature, culture, and philosophers at this time.

Political Ideology in the Roman Empire

In the patron-client system of the Roman Empire, there is a strong, visible divide between the strong and the weak that is maintained at all cost. The strong are born from nobility, educated, and gain access to political and economic powers.[1] They are elites and patrons under whom the weak, such

1. Paul's Letter to the First Corinthians displays a vast array of conflicting issues

as slaves, are put at the mercy of. Based on one's birth, social status, wealth, and power, honor is either bestowed to or shame is cast on an individual. While clients have to live under the benefaction of the patrons, their weak social position is perpetual. To perpetuate this divide between the strong the weak, the Roman political ideology or propaganda is ingrained on people's minds. The claim is that God ordains the emperor to be the father of all people; he is the provider of peace and security.[2] A person's duty is to submit fully to the Caesar, the divine son of God (*divi filius*). The cultural mood of this time is well known from the famous fable of Menenius Agrippa, which is used to support the idea of hierarchical unity in the Empire. Upon political unrest because of the Plebeians' revolt, Menenius tells this story to them:[3] One day all members of the body, such as hands and feet, rebelled against the belly, saying that they are not going to work any longer because the belly does nothing, but eats all the time. Then, the belly says, "That is okay. But know that if you do not work I will starve to death first and then you all as well." The point of Menenius is clear in that society as a body is one and should be maintained at all cost. The implication of this story can be put like this: "Do not complain about the hierarchical society or system and accept your place there and live your destined life as best as you can."

Because of this hierarchical worldview, those who are ignored most are slaves. In the Roman world, slaves are targets of ill treatment. The Roman novelist Chariton records the following horrible description of the crucifixion of a group of slaves:

> They were discovered and all securely fastened in the stocks for the night, and when day came the estate manager told Mithridates

---

largely due to class struggle. In fact, a majority of the Corinthian church members are from low class as we read in 1 Cor 1:26–29: "Consider your own call, brothers and sisters: not many of you were wise by human standards, not many were powerful, not many were of noble birth. But God chose what is foolish in the world to shame the wise; God chose what is weak in the world to shame the strong; God chose what is low and despised in the world, things that are not, to reduce to nothing things that are, so that no one might boast in the presence of God." But in the Corinthian church there are also a few wealthy members who may have exercised their privilege in the church; for example, as 1 Cor 11 shows, some wealthy members ate up all good food before the poor members came for the Lord's Supper. For more about conflicting issues in the Corinthian church, see Kim, *Christ's Body in Corinth*, 54–63. For a range of ideological issues (for example: identity, privilege, ritual and food) that cause the Corinthians to be in conflict or tension with each other, see Kim, *1 and 2 Corinthians*.

2. Kim, *Christ's Body in Corinth*, 39–53.
3. Livy, *History of Rome* 2.32.8–12.

what had happened. Without even seeing them or listening to their defence he immediately ordered the sixteen cell-mates to be crucified. They were duly brought out, chained together at foot and neck, each carrying his own cross. The executioners added this grim public spectacle to the requisite penalty as a deterrent to others so minded.[4]

Likewise, women are subordinate to men in such a divided world. This is because of such a long-standing view of gender hierarchy. See below for how it has been affected by classical philosophers such as Aristotle and Plato. As I wrote elsewhere:[5]

> Aristotle's view is similar to Plato's in the sense that both promote the hierarchical view of the cosmos and humans alike. Aristotle's worldview centers on *nous* (mind) as the divine element. Male is superior to female, woman being "a deformed male."[6] Man is "hot, fertile, perfectly formed and contributes soul to the generation of a new being; woman is cold, infertile, deformed and contributes the body."[7] In the world of Plato and Aristotle, there is no conception of equality between men and women, between Greeks and barbarians, between masters and slaves.[8] They show no concern for the weak of society. Rather, their philosophy contributes to cementing the structure of the status quo of the Greco-Roman world.

However, subordination of people is not limited to slaves or women. Rebels who fight against Rome are harshly treated or killed. Josephus records that Alexander Janneus, the Sadducean high priest in office during 103–76 BCE, crucified eight hundred Pharisees and watched their wives and children being slaughtered before their eyes.[9]

In summary, in the Roman Empire the weak such as the slaves and the poor are destined to serve the elites and society as a unified body. They are weak, physically and economically, and there is no way out of their destiny.

---

4. Chariton, *Chaireas and Callirhoe* 4.2.
5. Kim, *Christ's Body in Corinth*, 32.
6. Culianu, "Introduction: The Body Reexamined," 1–18. See also *Thraede*, 209.
7. Martin, *Corinthian Body*, 32.
8. Aristotle, *Politica* 1260a13.
9. Josephus, *Jewish Antiquities* 13.380–83; *Jewish War* 5.449–51.

Hellenistic Schools of Thought and View of Weakness

It is a daunting task to explore the view of "weakness" in Hellenistic schools of thought because there are many complex schools spanning a long period of time. So I will not attempt to cover all literature in the field concerning this issue, but will have a brief overview of various philosophical branches in the Roman Empire before and during Jesus' time. In order to explore a wide and deep sea of Hellenistic thought on weakness, I divide Hellenistic schools of thought into three big camps: Neopythagoreanism, Socrates and his heirs, and Hellenistic Judaism.

Neopythagoreanism

The origin of Neopythagoreanism, prominent in first and second centuries CE, goes back to Pythagoras (570–495 BCE), who influenced many Hellenistic philosophers including Socrates, Plato, and Aristotle.[10] Though Pythagoras himself did not leave any writings, his followers and commentators such as Parmenides, Empedocles, Philolaus, and Plato did so. His teaching and legacy are focused on science (mathematics) and esoteric teachings. His basic worldview may be summarized with the following two points: 1) the view that "the world is one" that was followed by the Stoics; 2) the transmigration of the souls (similar to reincarnation or to the immortality of the soul).[11] With these points it is necessary to purify the soul to get closer to the divine (leading to an emphasis on asceticism and vegetarianism). In the first and second centuries CE there is more emphasis on an ascetic life that ignores bodily pleasures.[12] The prominent figures in this time include Apollonius of Tyana (40–120 CE), who was a great teacher and miracle-worker like Jesus. His life was recorded in the *Life of Apollonius* by Philostratus (c. 170–c. 245 CE).[13]

Overall, Pythagoreanism emphasizes individual, inner experiences about the divine, and because of this, there is an early seed of dualism, which blossomed with Platonism (fourth century BCE) and later with

---

10. For an anthology of Pythagorean writings, see Guthrie, *Pythagorean Sourcebook and Library*. Regarding a life and thought of Pythagoras, see Gorman, *Pythagoras*; Stanley, *Pythagoras*.

11. See Laertius, viii, 36. See also Ferguson, *Backgrounds of Early Christianity*, 360–63.

12. Ferguson, *Backgrounds of Early Christianity*, 360–63.

13. Ibid.

Gnosticism, which then heavily influenced Christianity.[14] In dualism, the body is hopeless and only the soul is important and hopeful. Likewise, the body is weak and bad, and the soul is strong and good. Otherwise, there are no concerns about social ills in this world. A good life is possible by overcoming bodily desires and participating in the spiritual world. As we see here, this Pythagorean tradition about the human body and its weakness has permeated most western intellectual traditions even to this day.

Socrates and His Heirs (Plato, Aristotle, and Stoics)

Pythagoras influenced all of the following great philosophers in terms of the soul's search for a good life or happiness (*eudaimonia*): Socrates (c. 470–399 BCE), Plato (428–348 BCE), Aristotle (384–322 BCE), and the Stoics (Zeno, 335–263 BCE and his followers).[15] Though these philosophers are very different from each other, one thing they have in common is that their ethical explorations are based on self-focused virtue, which is believed to guarantee a good moral life. For Socrates knowledge is the main virtue by which individuals can attain happiness because strong will wins over secondary feeling/emotion and overcomes physical hardships.[16] He believes that a person equipped with the virtue of knowledge or wisdom has no fear of death because the soul does not perish—the view of the immortality of the soul. Overall, he believes that human reason, if rightly engaged and practiced, can overcome human predicaments of weakness that blocks happiness. In a way, he is very positive about human progress, based on reason-engaged knowledge that guides human souls to gain happiness beyond the body and this world.[17] For him weakness is a mere object to overcome by the virtue of knowledge.[18] Otherwise, there is not much discussion about human weakness or the human condition of weakness or the importance of a "weak" mind that suffers with others' agony.

Plato, a student of Socrates, writes about his teacher's teachings and interprets them from his perspective.[19] He believes that this world or

---

14. Ibid.

15. Ibid., 307–22; 333–47.

16. Brickhouse and Smith, *Socratic Moral Psychology*, 43–62. See also Cooper, *Reason and Emotion*, 3–75; *Pursuits of Wisdom*, 24–69.

17. Ferguson, *Backgrounds of Early Christianity*, 307–10.

18. Ibid.

19. Cooper, *Reason and Emotion*, 118–89; *Pursuits of Wisdom*, 70–143. See also

bodily life here on earth is a shadowy reality and that humans' ultimate goal is to follow the Idea (the Good) beyond this world.[20] His dualism is well known from his works: between the body and the soul, and between this world and the Idea. Similarly, he believes in the tripartite soul: reason, spirit, and appetite. Among these the most important part is reason, which should control the other two parts.[21] Because of this worldview, Plato, like his teacher, believes that human weakness can be overcome through reason or knowledge. He also argues that the ideal state should be ruled by philosopher-kings.[22] Because of this worldview, there is no place for Plato to engage in the world in terms of "weakness" because it can be overcome easily by reason or knowledge.

Aristotle, a student of Plato, differs from his teacher because he emphasizes both reason and virtuous action.[23] He argues that Plato's Idea or Form is insufficient to deal with ethics. In other words, reason alone cannot guarantee a good human life because there is a gap between the ideal (the Forms) and particular things in the world.[24] While Plato thinks particulars share the form, Aristotle rejects such an idea because particulars run on their own.[25] So he is critical of the cardinal virtues: wisdom or prudence (*phronesis*), justice (*dikaiosyne*), moderation (*sophrosyne*), and courage (*andreia*), which derive from Plato.[26] Before Plato, virtue (moral excellence) is understood mainly as intellectual capability or principle. That is, both Socrates and Plato believe that knowledge will liberate humans from the bondage of ignorance and weakness. But Aristotle distinguishes between practical virtues and intellectual virtues.[27] For example, in contrast to Plato, who believes that the only true *mimesis* (imitation) should be from the Good, Aristotle uses *mimesis* positively in a practical, moral sense that a person is born with an ability to imitate from others or nature: "Imitation is natural to man from childhood, one of his advantages over the lower

---

Ferguson, *Backgrounds of Early Christianity*, 310–15.

20. Irwin, *Plato's Ethics*, 169–297.

21. Plato, *Republic* 439–41. See also Ferguson, *Backgrounds of Early Christianity*, 315.

22. Plato, *Republic* 484–502.

23. Aristotle, *Nicomachean Ethics* Book 1.7. 1097a–1098b. See also Cooper, *Reason and Emotion*, 195–250; Ferguson, *Backgrounds of Early Christianity*, 318–22.

24. Ibid.

25. Ibid.

26. Plato, *Republic* 426–35.

27. Cooper, *Reason and Emotion*, 253–280.

animals being this, that he is the most imitative creature in the world, and learns at first by imitation. And it is also natural for all to delight in works of imitation."[28] Although Aristotle's view of ethics is more practical than his teacher, his overall basis in philosophy continues the tradition of reason and knowledge as we saw with Socrates and Plato. So basically, the same critiques apply to Aristotle.

Stoicism begins with Zeno (335–263 BCE) of Citium (Cyprus), whose main teaching focuses on the reason-controlled virtue, through which he believes humans can be happy.[29] Since feeling (*pathos*) is "a disturbance of the mind repugnant to Reason, and against Nature,"[30] happiness or good life must come from subduing the feeling.[31] That is, happiness does not have to do with wealth or external things, but has to do with self-control. He teaches that people can have peace of mind away from fear or disturbance in their lives. So much so he emphasizes indifference to the external things such as wealth or status. Accordingly, he advocates for the importance of self-control, right knowledge, and courage as means of overcoming weaknesses in human lives. So in Zeno's thinking, emotions are bad especially desire (*epithumia*), fear (*phobos*), pleasure (*hedone*), and pain (*lype*),[32] and he gives a corresponding counter-word to the first three: will (*boulesis*) against desire, caution (*eulabeia*) against fear, and joy (*chara*) against pleasure. But there is no remedy word for pain. Welborn suggests that this is perhaps because Stoics have no idea of how to deal with it. In his study of Paul's letters, Welborn argues that it is Paul who gives a right response to pain, namely the image of Christ crucified.[33] For Paul, on the one hand, Christ crucified poses a challenge to the powers, and on the other hand, it is a sign of God's presence with those who suffer now. Stoics, conversely, simply ignore it. Roman Stoics such as Cicero (106–43 BC) and Seneca (c. 3 BC–65 CE) stand in the same line of thought with Zeno and emphasize the importance of self-control.[34] They do not pay attention to pain or weak

---

28. Aristotle, *De Poetica*, 1448b. See also Ferguson, *Backgrounds of Early Christianity*, 318–322.

29. Inwood, "Introduction," 1–6. See also Brennan, *Stoic Life*, 3–45; Cooper, *Pursuits of Wisdom*, 144–225.

30. Cicero, *Tusculanae Quaestiones*, IV 6.

31. Brennan, "Stoic Moral Psychology," 257–94; *Stoic Life*, 51–113.

32. Cicero, *Tusculanae Quaestiones*, IV 6; Laertius, *Lives of the Philosophers* VII. 110.

33. See Welborn, "Paul and Pain," 547–70.

34. Algra, "Stoic Theology," 153–78.

people. According to Cicero, even slavery is understood as a matter of inner life: "Or look again at others, petty, narrow-minded men, or confirmed pessimists, or spiteful, envious, ill-tempered creatures, unsociable, abusive, and brutal; others again enslaved to the follies of love, impudent or reckless wanton, headstrong and yet irresolute, always changing their minds."[35] Likewise, Seneca emphasizes "inner self-control" and closes "his eyes to the external conditions of life"[36]:

> It is a mistake for anyone to believe that the condition of slavery penetrates into the whole being of a man. The better part of him is exempt. Only the body is at the mercy and disposition of a master; but the mind is its own master, and is so free and unshackled that not even this prison of the body, in which it is confined, can restrain it from using its own powers, following mighty aims, and escaping into the infinite to keep company with the stars. It is, therefore, the body that Fortune hands over to a master; it is this that he buys, it is this that he sells; that inner part cannot be delivered into bondage. All that issues from this is free; nor, indeed, are we able to command all things from slaves, nor are they compelled to obey us in all things; they will not carry out orders that are hostile to the state, and they will not lend their hands to any crime.[37]

As we see above, both Cicero and Seneca emphasize "inner virtues as true moral quality" and do not deal with the social conditions of life or injustices.[38] As a result, the status quo is not challenged. The rhetoric of *homonoia* (concord or unity) is more important than individual human dignity.[39]

In summary, what Socrates and his heirs have in common is as follows: 1) ethics is self-centered; 2) virtue is reason/knowledge-based; and 3) the aim of life is happiness (*eudamonia*). Otherwise, there is no serious discussion about the existence of weakness in the self, the community, and the world. Weakness is never considered a virtue. They believe social ills and individual problems can be solved through self-mastery of reason-based, self-focused ethics.

---

35. Cicero, *De finibus* 1.18.61.
36. Kim, *Christ's Body in Corinth*, 43.
37. Cicero, *De finibus* 1.18.61.
38. Kim, *Christ's Body in Corinth*, 44.
39. Regarding concord, see Chrysostom, *Discourses* 34.19; 38.11–14; 39.5. See also the fable of Menenius Agrippa's speech retold by Livy, *History of Rome* 2.32.8–12.

Hellenistic Judaism

Hellenistic Judaism is a diaspora Jewish intellectual movement that aims to secure the Jewish religious tradition by making appeals to Greek philosophy.[40] The principal voice in Hellenistic Judaism comes from Philo of Alexandria (c. 20 BC–40 CE), a Hellenistic Jewish philosopher, who argues that the Jewish God is equivalent to the Divine Logos.[41] Philo is a Platonist who often refers to Plato as "the most holy Plato."[42] He also employs Stoic doctrine and terminology, Aristotelian ethics, and Pythagorean ideas. Using these philosophical ideas, Philo protects Jewish tradition and even calls Moses's teachings "the summit of philosophy."[43] As a Platonist, Philo has a negative view about the material world and physical body.[44] The body is "an evil and a dead thing."[45] It is evil by nature and a blocker to the soul.[46] So he says, "Now, when we are alive, we are so though our soul is dead and buried in our body, as if in a tomb. But if it were to die, then our soul would live according to its proper life being released from the evil and dead body to which it is bound."[47] Philo also believes that human's ultimate goal is in the "knowledge of the true and living God."[48] Philo also adopts Plato's tripartite theory of soul: reason, spirit, and appetite, and places the origin of reason in God in the creation story in Gen 2:7, where God breathes into Adam "the breath of life."

Philo's ethical vision is similar to the Stoics. He believes that right virtue will lead humans to a good life. What matters is to follow the "path of right reason"[49] and the principles of nature such as wisdom, self-control, courage, and justice.[50] Like Stoics, Philo believes that a wise person "should imitate God who was impassible (*apathes*) hence the sage should achieve a state of *apatheia*, i.e., he should be free of irrational emotions (passions),

---

40. Ferguson, *Backgrounds of Early Christianity*, 450–54.
41. *De Ebrietate* 152.
42. *Quod Omnis Probus Liber Sit* 13.
43. *De Opificio Mundi* 8.
44. *De Specialibus Legibus* 3.1–6.
45. *Legum Allegoriarum* 3.72–74; *Gig.* 15.
46. *Legum Allegoriarum* 3.69.
47. *De Opificio Mundi* 67–69; *Legum Allegoriarum* 1.108.
48. *De Decalogo* 81; *De Abrahamo* 58; *De Praemiis et Poenis* 14.
49. *De Migratione Abrahami* 128.
50. *Legum Allegoriarum* 1.63–64. See also *De Abrahamo* 16; *De Opificio Mundi* 143; *De Specialibus Legibus* 2.13; 3.46–47, 112, 137; *De Virtutibus* 18.

pleasure, desire, sorrow, and fear, and should replace them by rational or well-reasoned emotions (*eupatheia*), joy, will, compunction, and caution. In such a state of *eupatheia*, the sage achieves a serene, stable, and joyful disposition in which he is directed by reason in his decisions."[51] As we have seen with Stoic philosophers, Philo also believed that there is no room to explore the concept of weakness in personal and communal lives, not to mention the positive effects of welcoming the weak.

In summary, Philo's moral vision and ethics is not very different from Plato other than his love and support for Judaism. As an elite, dualist philosopher, Philo does not acknowledge weakness in his life and believes that everything including all human frailty will be overcome by the power of reason/knowledge. Moreover, since the goal of life or ultimate salvation is not in this world, he does not need to address complex matters of society that involve weakness, whether personal or communal. In the end, we can say that Philo's Hellenistic Judaism differs from Jesus' Judaism with its higher view of this world. As we know from the Hebrew Bible, the main view of the world is not as negative as that seen in these Hellenistic worldviews. According to the creation story in Genesis, this world and humanity are created by God. At the end of the next chapter we will explore Jesus' view of Judaism and the law in relation to his context.

Summary

We have explored various ideologies about human nature, morality, and ethics in the Roman world. There is a clear divide between the ruler and the ruled. Resources are allocated based on social status, and the strong are served by the weak. In this Roman world, the dominant ruling philosophy is Stoicism whose ideal is hierarchical unity: "The world is unified with one ruler." For Hellenistic schools of thought, moral life is possible because of self-focused virtue ethics; otherwise there is not much exploration of the weakness-ridden world and humanity that needs salvation. So much so that weakness is not explored seriously. Their teaching is like this: "Regardless of what is happening outside of you, do not be bothered or controlled by it; find peace and tranquillity within you." Especially with Plato, the big problem is dualism between this world (as a copy of the Good) and the Idea. So the body is temporary and bad, and the goal of life is to purify the

---

51. http://www.iep.utm.edu/philo. See also *Quaestiones et Solutiones in Genesim* 2.57; *De Abrahamo* 201–4; *De Fuga et Inventione* 166–67; *De Migratione Abrahami* 67.

soul. Indifference to worldly matters is injected into people's mind, and as a result, the bodily needs and issues of human dignity in a hostile world are ignored and not addressed. Because of this dualism, the existence of the weak is taken for granted. Stoics even think the destiny of the weak is given by birth. They argue that slaves are born into their destiny and that the best life for them is to serve their masters without complaints. Overall, virtue ethics in this time does not address the problem of injustices coupled with the harsh rule of hierarchical unity. All it says is "You can control yourself and maintain happiness." This self-focused virtue ethics does not address the issue of community or human dignity in society as a whole.

3

The View of Weakness in Jewish Tradition

THIS CHAPTER EXAMINES THE view of weakness in the Jewish world. My attempt, however, is not to cover the full range of Jewish tradition and literature. I will limit coverage to the creation story in Genesis, Deuteronomic writings, prophetic writings, and first-century Judaism. Then we will touch on Jesus' view of weakness in comparison to the Jewish tradition, seeing both Jesus' continuity and discontinuity with that tradition.

View of Weakness in the Creation Story

The Hebrew Bible is a collection of various writings produced and edited for the need of communities in different times and contexts. It is not a single unified book that offers one view of God or of the world. The four identifiable sources are as follows: J (the Yawhistic source), E (the Eloistic source), D (the Deuteronomist source), and P (the priestly source). All this implies that each tradition can be studied on its own to seek earlier religious life of the community behind such a tradition.[1] Among these four, J and P are seen in the creation story of Genesis. J's theology or tradition begins in Gen 2:5b and it offers readers a sense of weakness embedded in human, as Yahweh forms *Adam* by taking the dust out of the ground (*Adamah*) and "breathes into his nostrils the breath of life (*nishmat chaim*)" (Gen 2:7). As a result, Adam becomes *nefesh* (the living being), which has a mixture of the heavenly and the earthly elements. From this mythic story about human nature, it is natural that humans die and return to earth: "By the sweat

---

1. Cassuto, *Documentary Hypothesis*.

of your face you shall eat bread until you return to the ground, for out of it you were taken; you are dust, and to dust you shall return" (Gen 3:19). Likewise, this idea of dust is followed by later biblical writers and becomes a symbol of human frailty (Ps 103:14): "For he knows how we were made; he remembers that we are dust" (cf. Gen 18:27; Job 4:19; 34:15; Ps 104:29; Eccl 3:20; 12:7). Similarly, it also refers to the grave (Ps 22:15, 29; 30:9; Dan 12:2). So the basic premise here is that humans are born weak and live in weakness.

In J's view, humans are embedded in weakness, whether it is physical or spiritual. The idea of the human comes with mixed elements: the spiritual element (breath of life), the earthly weak element (dust), and the combined life of *nefesh* (living being). This view of the J tradition is very pertinent to our understanding of true humanity. That is, we are strong *and* weak. That is who we are as the *nefesh*. The insight here is that we have to find strength in the midst of or through weakness. Through weakness we know and feel what strength must be like. Through the prism of the weakness we can see others' faces as they are and feel what they feel.

In this anthropology of the J tradition even God is human-like (anthropomorphic): God feels and acts like humans. Such a God is never remote but immanent with people. This God is very down-to-earth, attending to the human world. God is not the Idea or an absolute being that cannot be moved. Rather, God is weak in some sense because God is involved in the complexities of the human world. J's view of God and humanity helped one to deal with his or her community. Today we need to be informed by this kind of anthropology and theology because it helps us deal with who we are.

In J's view of theology God appears to be weak in that God regrets making humankind: "And the LORD (Yahweh) was sorry that he had made humankind on the earth, and it grieved him to his heart" (Gen 6:6). in this way God's anthropomorphism, one of the signature characteristics in J's theology, is evident. God also smells "the pleasing odor" (Gen 8:21). God "walks about in the garden" (Gen 3:8) and "goes down" to see what is happening on earth (Gen 11:5; 18:21). These anthropomorphic expressions and descriptions about God are widespread in the Hebrew Bible.[2] In all of this the point is that J's God engages with the world of weakness.

---

2. For example: Exod 33:23; Isa 6:1; Num 7:89; Ps 132:13; 135:21; Dan 7:9; also the songs in Exod 15 and 2 Sam 22; Ps 18.

The other source P (Priestly source) begins in Gen 1:1. This tradition originates with the priestly class in fifth century BCE, after the Babylonian exile. As conveyed in the first creation account in Genesis 1, P emphasizes God's majestic creation and transcendence. God creates by speaking the word and does so in orderly fashion, beginning with light and ending with creation of humans. God is all powerful and majestic and does not need to get his hands dirty. God is above humanity and yet humans are the very reflection/image of him (Gen 1:27). There is a strong divide between God and humanity, though humans are a reflection of God. P's God remains strong and is worshipped through law and order, which echoes the Stoics' emphasis on *homonoia* (concord). This view of P reflects the post-exilic concerns about God's punishment as experienced in Babylon. In this context, law observance, rituals, and purity are crucial matters to the future of Israel. As a corollary, there is a strong boundary between the chosen and the profane as we see in Ezra and Nehemiah.

As we get hints from above, P's anthropology or theology is tilted to one side, which is that human weakness is not reflected very much in the humanity. Obviously, a good part of P's contribution to our understanding of anthropology or theology is that we humans are lofty beings from the beginning; to say, we are created in the image of God. That is good, but the problem is how we can understand a complex image of who we are in relation to the image of God. In sum, if we want to emphasize human loftiness with God's creation, we also have to include the "dusty" part of human nature as expressed in J. This kind of insight is closer to our experience in our daily lives than an insulated spiritual stronghold apart from the weakness, be it bodily or not.[3] If we acknowledge we are not perfect, that is, we are weak, we can face others with a kindred mindset; we are not very different in kind and share with others more similarities than differences.

---

3. The more realistic life experience is that we go through stormy days and yet see clear skies soon. Life is never always full of sunny days. Life in the world needs rain and sun. This kind of human experience is explored in my recent book, *A Transformative Reading of the Bible*, where I identify three moments of life: "I am no-one," "I am someone," and "I am one-for-other," all of which are critical to human transformation. In this book, for example, I explore Hannah's difficult life experience and develop the three-phase human transformation. In the end, Hannah can be a better person because of her experience of weakness. Her marginal identity is conducive to her strength.

Deuteronomistic Works

Deuteronomistic History is a term coined by Martin Noth, who argues that Deuteronomy, Joshua, 1–2 Samuel, and 1–2 Kings are the work of a single author in the sixth century BCE when Jerusalem fell and Jewish leaders were taken into Babylonian exile. Using sources available to him, this author and historian rewrote a history about Judah with heavy-handed theological concern for God's law. In this history, God makes a covenant with Israel in the form of suzerain treaty. The law is given through Moses and should be kept because they were a people chosen. God promises to give the Israelites the Promised Land. But people were not obedient to the law of God, worshiping idols. So God punishes them with the use of the Assyrians and the Babylonians. Israel was defeated in 721 BCE, and subsequently, Judah in 586 BCE. Not to repeat the same mistake and punishment, the Deuteronomistic historian emphasizes the centralization of the cultic place in Jerusalem and strict observance of the Mosaic Law and covenant. As a result, law and order is emphasized; those who keep the law will prosper, and those who do not keep the law will perish. This is a system of reward and punishment.

In this Deuteronomistic school there is a strong sense of renewal of Judaism through a return to the Mosaic covenant. As part of this school's reform program, humanitarian laws in the Law Codes defend the rights of the poor, widows, and orphans, including the resident aliens.[4] So God is understood as the one who cares for the marginalized. Deuteronomy 10:17–19 says: "For the LORD your God is God of gods and Lord of lords, the great God, mighty and awesome, who is not partial and takes no bribe, who executes justice for the orphan and the widow, and who loves the strangers, providing them food and clothing. You shall also love the stranger, for you were strangers in the land of Egypt." Deuteronomy 24: 17–21 is more specific about how to help them:

> You shall not deprive a resident alien or an orphan of justice; you shall not take a widow's garment in pledge. . . . When you reap your harvest in your field and forget a sheaf in the field, you shall not go back to get it; it shall be left for the alien, the orphan, and the widow, so that the LORD your God may bless you in all your

---

4. For an extensive review of poverty in the Hebrew Bible, see Wafawanaka, *Am I Still My Brother's Keeper?* Humanitarian laws are contained in the Covenant Code (Exod 20:19—23:33), the Deuteronomic Code (Deut 12–26), and the Holiness Code (Lev 17–26). See also Worthington, *Reading the Bible in an Age of Crisis*.

undertakings. . . . When you beat your olive trees, do not strip what is left; it shall be for the alien, the orphan, and the widow. . . . When you gather the grapes of your vineyard, do not glean what is left; it shall be for the alien, the orphan, and the widow.

But it must be said that Deuteronomic History writings do not provide a perfect, ideal model for the transformation of society. There is a strong tendency towards monotheism that denies other cultures and religions. Laws and regulations are often added to maintain a strict unified state. Monarchy and slavery are legitimate in this school of thought. Aliens, widows, and orphans are helped through charity, but they do not fully participate in society. Slaves should be treated well by laws, but they are still slaves unless they are freed. In the end, Deuteronomic writings have a double standard that the weak are protected even in limited ways and that they never fully participate in society as equal members.

Prophetic Writings

No part of the Hebrew Bible is more concerned with social justice than the prophetic writings, especially the Book of Amos. Prophetic writings in general are very critical of the rich's manipulation of the poor because God is a God of the poor and the marginalized. After the Davidic monarchy,[5] society becomes more stratified, and disparity among people is larger than before. The rich and powerful abuse the poor. Amos challenges the rich:

> They who trample the head of the poor into the dust of the earth, and push the afflicted out of the way; father and son go in to the same girl, so that my holy name is profaned. (Amos 2:7)

---

5. The establishment and development of Davidic monarchy itself involves royal ideology and a stratified society. David, as new king of the unified Israel, needs a strong government with a foundational narrative about his regime. Yawhists (J) help him by prohibiting different voices regarding scripture or cultic place, providing legitimacy to the Davidic monarchy by connecting Abraham's covenant with David, twelve sons of Jacob with twelve tribes of Israel. David is also hailed as the stalwart messiah through whom the Davidic royal house is blessed forever. But soon his unified kingdom began to fall because it was established by military power and central government that does not take care of the poor and the weak. Lord Acton's warning speaks a lot in this regard: "Power tends to corrupt and absolute power corrupts absolutely."

> Hear this word, you cows of Bashan who are on Mount Samaria, who oppress the poor, who crush the needy, who say to their husbands, "Bring something to drink!" (Amos 4:1)
>
> Therefore because you trample on the poor and take from them levies of grain, you have built houses of hewn stone, but you shall not live in them; you have planted pleasant vineyards, but you shall not drink their wine. (Amos 5:11)
>
> Hear this, you that trample on the needy, and bring to ruin the poor of the land . . . buying the poor for silver and the needy for a pair of sandals, and selling the sweepings of the wheat. (Amos 8:4, 6)

Amos rejects the claim of the powerful people who wait for the day of the Lord, and sarcastically pokes at them: "Alas for you who desire the day of the Lord! Why do you want the day of the Lord? It is darkness, not light" (Amos 5:18). The day of the Lord must be the day that "justice rolls down like waters, and righteousness like an ever-flowing stream" (Amos 5:24). Amos delivers the oracle of God: "I hate, I despise your festivals, and I take no delight in your solemn assemblies. Even though you offer me your burnt offerings and grain offerings, I will not accept them; and the offerings of well-being of your fatted animals I will not look upon. Take away from me the noise of your songs; I will not listen to the melody of your harps" (Amos 5:20–23). Without justice for the poor and the weak, no offerings or sacrifices will be accepted by God. Animals are killed and offered at an altar as an act of repentance for God. The killing of an animal and burnt offering is symbolic in that what is really needed is people's change of their mind. Atonement does not happen because of the rituals done. It would be silly to believe that sins are cleansed and transferred to animals because of the scapegoats on the Yom Kippur. But apparently, many believed this to be true. That is a serious distortion of true religiosity required by such a law and practice of atonement. The word of repentance in the Hebrew Bible is *shub*, which means "to turn to" God. To correct a ritual-centered mind Jeremiah asks, "Circumcise yourselves to the Lord" (Jer 4:4). At the absence of justice and righteousness in society, Jeremiah offers a sharp and yet realistic remedy to the problem: "Circumcise yourselves to the Lord, remove the foreskin of your hearts" (Jer 4:4a). Interestingly, Paul also echoes Jeremiah's social critique coupled with his deep spirituality in Romans:

"Real circumcision is a matter of the heart; it is spiritual and not literal" (Rom 2:29).[6] The fundamental solution starts with the human heart, which will direct all other things, whether personal or communal. The issue is that people do not break their hearts, which were hardened enough not to see the suffering of others. For Jeremiah physical circumcision or appearance of religious ritual is not the issue. So he delivers the word of the Lord that speaks about a new covenant not based on the laws written on the stone but on their hearts. See Jer 31:31–33:

> The days are surely coming, says the LORD, when I will make a new covenant with the house of Israel and the house of Judah. It will not be like the covenant that I made with their ancestors when I took them by the hand to bring them out of the land of Egypt—a covenant that they broke, though I was their husband, says the LORD. But this is the covenant that I will make with the house of Israel after those days, says the LORD: I will put my law within them, and I will write it on their hearts; and I will be their God, and they shall be my people.

As for Amos the real issue is not that there are poor people who need food and shelter or that the rich do not care about them, but that the rich and elites do not understand what God wants: justice and righteousness.[7] Because God is righteous and just, people have to follow him in their mind and heart. Namely, the issue is not simply a matter of charity but a matter of theology and ethics. The poor must be taken care of not only because they are poor but because they are God's children. In a way, the weakness of the poor should be part of the rich's mind. This is exactly where Jeremiah joins Amos in critiquing their unspiritual way of life focused on rituals and festivals. In Jeremiah's spirituality as well as in Paul's, what is most important is the circumcision of the heart that responds to the agony of others. Rituals or festivals that do not have embodied lives for the weak are void or noisy gongs.

---

6. I extensively explored Paul's personal and political transformation with this insight on spiritual circumcision. See Kim, *Transformative Reading of the Bible*, 67–82.

7. Micah says similar things that God requires of his people: "O mortal, what is good; and what does the Lord require of you but to do justice, and to love kindness, and to walk humbly with your God" (Micah 6:8).

First-Century Judaism

Josephus lists four sects in Palestine in the first century CE indicating that Judaism is not unified at this time. We will review these four sects briefly and explore Jesus' relationship with them. First, the Sadducees were wealthy aristocrats who ran the Temple. They did not believe in the resurrection of the dead (Matt 22:23; Mark 12:18–27). In a sense, they would not need resurrection in the future because they have a resurrection-like life now with power and wealth. On the other hand, if resurrection takes place in the future, they would be in fear that they would lose everything that they had. So they could not accept the oral Torah which challenged their status.

Second, in contrast to the Sadducees, the Pharisees believe in the resurrection and accept both the oral and written Torah. They are law-based reformers who emphasize the strict observance of the law. Although their interpretation of the law is strict, their intention should not be doubted because they are concerned with the renewal of Judaism and people's lives. In other words, their teaching was well accepted by the populace. Even Jesus acknowledges their good teaching: "Therefore, do whatever they teach you and follow it" (Matt 23:3a). Even though the Pharisees are mainly portrayed as hypocrites in the Gospels (Mark 7:5–7; Matt 15:1–3; 23:1–5; 13–39), historically speaking they are not hypocrites. The negative portrayal of the Pharisees is probably due to the later evangelists aiming to elevate Jesus above the Pharisees. But in fact, as several references in the Gospels indicate, Jesus' relationship with the Pharisees is not always confrontational. Some Pharisees showed hospitality to Jesus, inviting him for a meal (Luke 7:36; 11:37; 14:1). In John, there were secret believers (Nicodemus and Joseph Arimathea) who had sympathy with Jesus. Others warned Jesus of an impending danger by Herod (Luke 13:30–31). The real contentious issue between the Pharisees and Jesus was a matter of interpretation of the law. The Pharisees did not have much flexibility about the law and keep the law rigorously. Their argument could be described in this way: "Yes, the weak or the poor have to be taken care of, but the work of caring should not be done on the Sabbath. Law keeping is more important than loving others." The Pharisees thought of themselves as experts in the Law and their knowledge was sufficient enough to lead people toward God. All others who do not agree with them were weak and hopeless.

In sum, though the Pharisees have genuine love for God, their interpretation of the Law is strict and often blinded. That is a problem. Though they have love for the poor and the weak, their love for them is conditional.

Because of this, there is a logic of "either/or"—between those who stick to their teaching and those who do not. There is no room for embracing the weak or the marginalized without conditions. Because of their confidence in their interpretation of the Law, they believe they are strong. This view of the Pharisees resembles that of the Stoics who also emphasize law and order, as we have seen before.

Third, the Essenes are sectarians who withdrew to the desert called Qumran with distaste towards the Jerusalem Temple and its leadership. They established their own community and interpreted the scriptures, expecting their own messiahs.[8] They were radical apocalypticists who anticipated the soon-to-happen judgment of God. Because of this, they were not concerned with this world's peace or justice. They were sectarians who believed that they were the only heirs of God's people. Their worldview was negative in the sense that they did not expect to transform people and the world, as the Pharisees did. There were no concerns for the poor or the weak.

Lastly, the Fourth Philosophy was the name for the group of people who actively sought independence for Israel by rising against the political powers. They believed that the kingdom of God and liberation of Israel should come through all possible ways, including military might. Their strategy for liberation of people from Rome was realistic because Rome would not withdraw otherwise. Liberation of people requires direct military resistance against Rome. This was a strategy of "eye for eye" reminiscent of the retaliation laws in Exod 21:22–25.[9]

Jesus' View of Weakness

Jesus lived in first-century Galilee where Hellenism and Jewish traditions coexisted.[10] As we saw above, Jesus does not seem to belong to a particular sect that Josephus mentions. However, he seems to get closer to the Pharisees even though his relationship with them is strained.[11] He shares with them the central belief about God's covenant with Israel. Both the Pharisees

---

8. Collins, "A Messiah before Jesus?" 15–35.

9. For more about the retaliation laws, see Kim, "*Lex Talionis* in Exod 21:22–25."

10. Freyne, *Jesus Movement and Its Expansion*, 13–55.

11. For discussion about Jesus' possible relationships with the Pharisaic tradition, see Wild, "Encounter between Pharisaic and Christian Judaism," 105–24. See also Culbertson, "Changing Christian Images," 539–61; "Pharisaic Jesus and His Parables," 74–77.

and Jesus share the importance of the Law, as Jesus clearly says in Matt 5:17: "Do not think that I have come to abolish the law or the prophets; I have come not to abolish but to fulfill." But their interpretation of the Law is not the same. Jesus breaks away from the Pharisees' rigid interpretation of the law, especially regarding purity or sabbatical laws and interprets the law flexibly in view of the spirit of the law, which has to do with restoration of life. Namely, for Jesus, saving lives is more important than the mere keeping of the law. Likewise, Jesus is not interested in dividing humans into the good and the bad or the strong and the weak, since all are the children of God who need his grace and opportunity. He eats with sinners because the social outcasts or sinners also belong to God's house.

Otherwise, Jesus does not get close to the teaching of other sects such as the Sadducees or Essenes. Unlike the Sadducees, Jesus challenges the dominant powers that block God's rule. Since Jesus engages in the world, he is very different from the sectarian group of Essenes. Though some suggest that Jesus was a revolutionary who was interested in overthrowing Rome and establishing his own kingdom with his twelve disciples that symbolically represent twelve tribes ruling in the future Messianic Kingdom of Israel, this reading does not gain much support because of a lack of evidence.[12] Jesus rather "led a nonviolent anti-Roman movement that became very popular and dangerous to Romans and their quislings."[13] Jesus as God's representative claims that God is king, not the Roman emperor. It is possible that people want to make Jesus their king, but it is doubtful that Jesus claims his own kingship.[14]

---

12. Aslan, *Zealot*. Aslan argues that Jesus was a Zealot, based on Jesus asked his disciples to buy a sword (Luke 22:36), and earlier he said two swords would be enough (Luke 22:38); He did not come to bring peace but a sword (Matt 10:34). But his conclusion is the hasty one. Jesus' saying in Luke 22:36 ("And the one who has no sword must sell his cloak and buy one") may be understood symbolically in that Jesus warns his disciples of hostile and difficult times ahead. But his disciples misunderstand Jesus and respond to Jesus that they have two swords, gearing up for fighting (22:38). Then, Jesus retorts back to them, saying "it is enough" (*hikanon estin*); in other words, Jesus does not say that the two swords are enough for battle. The subject of "to be enough" is the third person singular neutral ("it"), which does not refer to the two swords. Rather, Jesus plainly says "Enough of this talk: drop this subject." See Craddock, *Luke*, 260. See also Fitzmyer, *Gospel according to Luke*, 1432–34. Fitzmyer states: "The irony concerns not the number of weapons, but the mentality of the apostles. Jesus will have nothing to do with swords, even for defence" (1434).

13. Charlesworth, *Historical Jesus*, 108.

14. Kim, *Resurrecting Jesus*, 46–47.

In sum, Jesus inherits prophetic teaching and wisdom from the Jewish prophets, especially Jeremiah, Hosea, and Amos. His concerns for the marginalized are an obvious driving force behind his teaching and ministry. Jesus does not approach them merely from a "compassion" ministry perspective because he does not merely identify with them. As we will see in the next chapter, Jesus himself experiences various aspects of weakness, whether personal or communal. Accordingly, Jesus' definition or view of weakness must be different. As we have seen in Hellenistic philosophies, the dominant view of weakness is negative and it is something that must be overcome. Likewise, the dominant form of virtue has to do with overcoming weakness: wisdom or prudence (*phronesis*), justice (*dikaiosyne*), moderation (*sophrosyne*), and courage (*andreia*).[15] The culture says that the strong are honorable, and that the weak are shameful. So much so, power/honor comes from birth (family background), education (four virtues in the above), and wealth. But Jesus' understanding of weakness is different; it can be part of virtue and the source of strength. For Jesus honor is gained not by overpowering others but through empowering them. To do so requires the eyes of weakness that we explored before.[16]

Jesus' view of weakness is that "we are weak *and* strong." It is not that "we are weak but strong." This latter view comes from a dominant cultural perspective of the divide between the strong and the weak. According to Jesus, what is required for us is not to act like a weak person but to recognize our weakness, physically, psychologically, spiritually, and communally. The truly "weak" people are strong because they know who they are before God and the world. In this regard, the human problem is that we refuse our weakness and seek strength without going through weakness. In Jesus' view, the problem of the strong people has to do with their denial of weakness in the world; they are strong without God and do not have a heart for the weak. In other words, the issue is that their hearts are hardened and disillusioned by their power because they think that they are strong. In

---

15. Plato, *Republic* 426–35.

16. This view of Jesus is seen with Paul, who adamantly says to those who think they are strong in Corinth: "God's foolishness is wiser than human wisdom, and God's weakness is stronger than human strength" (1 Cor 1:25). Here Paul refutes the strong Corinthians' perspective that they are wise or strong without knowing about their weakness before God and the world and without participating in Christ's death. Though Paul did not follow Jesus as disciple, his theology or thought about Jesus makes us wonder that he was a genuine interpreter of Jesus. The view of weakness and strength is such a place that they both have in common.

Jesus' view, we can become morally excellent insofar as we maintain such a stance of weakness. How one thinks about the weakness is kind of a litmus test through which we know there is a life of strength.

Summary

Thus far we have sketched the view of weakness in the Hebrew Bible and first-century Judaism. In the creation story in Genesis we identified two different views of God: the Yawhistic source (J) and the priestly source (P). The conclusion is that we need both views in tension. While J's God seems to be weak and down-to-earth, P's God is orderly and transcendent. We also examined the Deuteronomistic codes and the prophetic writings and found that God is the God of the poor and the weak. But we also pointed out that the God portrayed in the Deuteronomistic codes appears to be the God of reward and punishment. Prophetic writings deal with social justice because the poor are left uncared for and their rights are ignored. Finally, we have seen the diversity of first-century Judaism and briefly touched on Jesus' view of weakness, which will be fully explored in the next chapters.

4

Jesus' Experience and Interpretation of Weakness

HUMAN BEINGS ARE INFLUENCED by external conditions such as family background and social environment and respond to experiences in their lives. Jesus is not an exception to this. Therefore any portrait of Jesus that deprives him of his humanity is not simply wrong, but naïve and shallow. Jesus was a first-century CE Jew, born in a particular place (Nazareth rather than Bethlehem) through particular parents, grew up in Nazareth, and lived a life of insecurity as a *tekton*.[1] Otherwise, as soon as Jesus is theologized as a divine Son from the perspective of Trinity or from the literal incarnation in that God became Jesus, our understanding about his life and work would be shallow at best or mistaken. Why is this so? First of all, the idea of deity-becoming-human is a myth that is found widespread across religions and cultures. When Augustus is divinized as the son of God, people in his empire are supposed to know that he is still a human being, not the son of God in literal sense.[2] When Jesus is called Immanuel, it simply means that God is present through Jesus' life or work. That is the language of faith. People see and experience the love of God through Jesus' work.[3] That is incarnation theology to which we will turn in a moment.

Second, in the Synoptic Gospels the primary image of Jesus is as the Son of God who does the work of God. The Son of God is a human agent

---

1. As I will argue later, a *tekton* job does not provide Jesus with a decent life that satisfies the need of his family.

2. For an extensive study of the "son of God" figure in the Roman world, see Peppard, *The Son of God in the Roman World*.

3. Kim, *Truth, Testimony, and Transformation*, 28–46.

in the Hebrew Bible; it can be Israel as a whole, and it can be particular individuals who work for God (king, prophet, or priest). Jesus fits well in the category of prophets since he advocates for the marginalized. Regardless of what Jesus thought of himself, the title "Son of God" is not a divine title at all. Even today if I say, "I am the son of God," no one would think I am divine. I use this term to state that I belong to God and work for him like a son.

Third, even in John's Gospel the idea of incarnation should not be taken literally. In the Prologue (John 1:1–18), the first fourteen verses introduces the Logos to readers, and Jesus is not mentioned until verse 14, where Jesus is implied: "The Logos became flesh, and dwelled among us." "The Logos became flesh" is an expressive statement of incarnation in that the invisible Logos (reason, word, spirit, or wisdom) became manifest with the visible form in this world. The flesh as metaphor may refer to this vulnerable world where Jesus was born. In other words, the flesh should include both this world and Jesus who shows who God is there. The flesh also represents a life of somebody in that particular world. This understanding is what I call the "metaphorical incarnation" as opposed to the "literal incarnation."[4] Whereas the latter equates the Logos with Jesus, the former distinguishes between the Logos and Jesus. In my interpretation, Jesus embodies the Logos. If we are not clear about this distinction, we tend to think that every good thing is possible with Jesus because it is Jesus, who is God. With this tendency salvation is possible because of this strong divine Jesus who took the side of the voiceless and was crucified in weakness. Similarly, Jesus suffered and God also co-suffered with Jesus for the salvation of humanity. But the question is: Why does God require such an innocent death of Jesus? Could human suffering be good and necessary for human salvation?

Fourth, Jesus is followed by many, not because he was divine, but because he was a faithful son of God who loved God and the world until he died on the cross. If we eliminate this bare fact of his life, we are not different from the Gnostics who deny the humanity of Jesus. While people celebrate his life and death, they rarely connect the tragic aspects of his death with the evil hands behind it. Likewise, they never imagine Jesus' weakness or the weakness that he endures in a harsh world. They just say hallelujah because he died instead of them.

Fifth, Paul, one of the important early Christian voices, recognizes the humanity of Jesus and yet offers a new perspective about him in 2 Cor

---

4. Ibid.

5:16: "From now on, therefore, we regard no one from a human point of view; even though we once knew Christ from a human point of view, we know him no longer in that way." "From a human point of view" means that Jesus was a human like others. Paul does not deny Jesus' humanity. What he says here is that his perspective about Jesus has changed: "We know him no longer in that way." This is the language of faith that does not deny the humanity of Jesus and yet gives a new meaning. After this, Paul states what it means to be a new-perspective person: "So if anyone is in Christ, there is a new creation: everything old has passed away; see, everything has become new!" (2 Cor 5:17). In this verse, Paul's emphasis is on "in Christ" (*en christo*), which is a mode of life like Jesus. If anyone follows this way of life, he or she is a new creation. Actually, Paul's view of Jesus is focused on a much larger, soteriological perspective that "in Christ God was reconciling the world to himself" (2 Cor 5:19).

Jesus' Experience of Weakness

There are a number of locations where Jesus experienced weakness, whether personal or communal. To begin with, the location of Jesus' experience of weakness has to do with his hometown, Nazareth of Galilee.[5] Galilee is known for its peasant uprisings and is a place of resistance against the dominant systems—the harsh Roman rules and local elites' economic exploitation.[6] Galilee is one of the most isolated regions in Judea.[7] Galilee was poor and was looked down upon by Jerusalem.[8] In this social economic

---

5. Matthew and Luke connect Jesus' birthplace with Bethlehem to emphasize that Jesus is the Jewish Messiah (Micah 5:1). David's anointing in Bethlehem (1 Sam 16:1–13) is a model for Jesus, who is born there as the Son of David. But Mark does not have a birth narrative at all and clearly says that Jesus is from Nazareth of Galilee (Mark 1:9). Interestingly, even in Matthew and Luke, Bethlehem disappears in the entire narrative after Jesus' birth.

6. See Horsley, *Jesus and Empire*, 35–54. For a major overview of the time of Jesus, see Hanson and Oakman, *Palestine in the Time of Jesus*. See also Oakman, *Political Aims of Jesus*.

7. For an overview of life in Galilee, see Horsley, *Archaeology, History, and Society in Galilee*; Hanson and Oakman, *Palestine in the Time of Jesus*. See also Crossan, *Birth of Christianity*, 209–35; *Excavating Jesus*, 136–223. See also Moxnes, "Identity in Jesus' Galilee," 390–416. Moxnes argues that "Viewed from the perspective of intersectionality the system of domination by Herod Antipas and the Galilean elite as reflected in the Gospels reveals multiple and interrelated forms of oppression" (408).

8. See Horsley, *Jesus and Empire*. See also Oakman, *Political Aims of Jesus*.

environment, Jesus may have had a "cognitive dissonance"—a psychological conflict between his belief about God and the reality with which he is faced. His belief tells him that God must rule the world with peace and justice, but what happens to the world is the opposite of his belief. People in Galilee and elsewhere suffer from all kinds of anomalies in society, a form of lack of God's rule. Jesus must have struggled because of this. In this dire situation of despair and destruction of lives, most people choose a life of silence and stay where they are without resistance against the evil system or people. The terrible situation of life permeates all parts of Palestine. This is a context where Jesus is led to proclaim God's rule, not Rome's rule, by asking for a change of mind. In other words, his concern is about God's reign now and his dream is to provide "a changed life" for people.[9]

Nazareth of Galilee is only a few miles south of Sepphoris, which is, according to Josephus, "the ornament of all Galilee" and "the strongest city in Galilee."[10] This city was heavily armed with Roman forces and shows the splendor of both residential and recreational buildings as well as its luxurious lifestyle, in contrast with the life of other parts of Galilee.[11] It may be true then that, as the Gospel narrative suggests, Jesus went to areas other than Sepphoris in his public ministry such as Nazareth, Capernaum, Cana, Bethsaida, Chorazin, and Nain and subsequently taught "the peasants in the towns and villages" (Luke 8:1; Mark 1:38).[12] Scholars are left to wonder why Jesus did not go to Sepphoris and Tiberias, the new capital of Galilee in 20 CE, during his public ministry. Though we do not know whether Jesus ever taught there, it may be inferred that Sepphoris was not Jesus' priority and therefore was neglected.

What does it mean for Jesus to live as a Jew born and raised in Nazareth of Galilee, only a few miles south of Sepphoris, which is the capital of Galilee—a most gorgeous, luxurious Roman city rebuilt by Herod Antipas? Jesus may have even visited this imperial city Sepphoris, looking for or finding a menial job there. Jesus must have seen all kinds of local village people nad neighbors living uner life-breaking circumstances due to famine or the elites' economic exploitation.

9. Keck argues that the "kingdom's primary import was moral—i.e., a changed life." *Who is Jesus?* 85.

10. Josephus, *Jewish Antiquities* xviii, 27.

11. Freyne, *Jesus, a Jewish Galilean*, 144. For the impact of Sepphoris and Tiberias on the Galilean economy, see Reed and Crossan, *Excavating Jesus*, 151–53, 204–6; Fredriksen, *Jesus of Nazareth*, 182.

12. Culpepper, "Contours of the Historical Jesus," 73.

Second, the location of Jesus' experience of weakness has to do with his parental background. Historically speaking, Jesus may have been born illegitimately through a nameless father with whom Mary had relationships (details about which can be hardly known).[13] Jesus' biological father is unknown and Jesus is called the "son of Mary" (Mark 6:3), which is very unusual given the fact that in Jewish tradition a child is referred to as the son or daughter of a father.[14] Interestingly, in John 8:41, Jews respond to Jesus, saying: "We were not born of fornication," "as if to imply, as *you* were."[15] Joseph married Mary and was believed to adopt Jesus without hesitation. Then we do not know when Joseph died because after the birth story he disappears in the narrative. It is possible that Jesus grew up even without Joseph. The implication is that Jesus' childhood seemed abnormal and lonely because of this parental background. For example, his village people may have looked down upon him, calling him "the son of Mary" from Nazareth. Jesus was also looked down upon by his village people: "Is not this the *tekton* the son of Mary and brother of James and Joses and Judas and Simon, and are not his sisters here with us?" (Mark 6:3).

Third, the location of Jesus' experience of weakness also has to do with his upbringing. Jesus grew up with Mary, single mother, if Joseph died early enough. Though we do not know details about Jesus' relationships to his siblings, there is a clue in Mark 3:31–32 that he, unlike an ordinary Jewish man in society, does not support the traditional family and states, "Whoever does the will of God is my brother and sister and mother" (Mark 3:35). Jesus refuses to speak to his family members when they look for him (Mark 3:31–35) and says to a crowd, "Who are my mother and my brothers?" (Mark 3:33; cf. Matt 12:48). I think Jesus' radical view of family may

---

13. Kim, *Resurrecting Jesus*, 32. In general, the virgin birth or miraculous birth story is a technique that explains a hero's greatness in ancient literature. For example, the birth accounts of Plato, Alexander the Great, Augustus, and Pythagoras involve some kind of miraculous birth. See Cartlidge and Dungan, *Documents for the Study of the Gospels*, 129–36. But in Matthew's birth account, we see more than such a miraculous birth by the Holy Spirit. That is, Joseph engaged to Mary wants to break away from her because of her "mysterious" pregnancy (Matt 1:19). This telling tension conveyed in the birth story hints that Mary got pregnant with someone other than Joseph, her betrothed. Perhaps it is not an accident that Matthew takes the time explaining this. Interestingly, Matthew mentions four women in his genealogy who are of questionable moral character. See Schaberg, *Illegitimacy of Jesus*, 33. Finally, Joseph takes her as she is because of God's will that her pregnancy is done through the Holy Spirit (Matt 1:20).

14. Kim, *Resurrecting Jesus*, 31–32.

15. See Tabor, "A Historical Look: Part 4."

have alienated him from his family and village, as his rough relationships with them are indicated in Mark (for example: 3:20–21, 31–35; 6:1–6a).[16] Critical scholars claim this as a case for the "criterion of embarrassment," according to which Jesus' relationships with his family members are likely true because the evangelists and later editors of the Jesus traditions would not want to create such a negative story about Jesus and his family. Given all of this, it may be inferred that Jesus grew up lonely even though he had sisters and brothers (Mark 6:3). In fact, what truly distinguished and further alienated him from others may have been his ability to think profoundly about God's rule in the world, which goes beyond blood ties or kinship.

Fourth, the location of Jesus' experience of weakness has to do with his poverty. How do we know he was poor? The first clue is his occupation of *tekton* (Mark 6:3), which is not a decently skilled job like a carpenter today but a manual worker using wood or stone. Jesus himself must be a *tekton* as opposed to Matthew's account where Jesus is referred to as the son of *tekton* Joseph (Matt 13:55). Matthew was probably embarrassed by the fact that Jesus was a *tekton* because the image of Jesus as the glorious son of God is not a good fit with that job. In Matthew, the principal characterization of Jesus is kingly. Jesus was born as the king of Jews and the Son of David. The magi visit the baby Jesus. So it is understandable that Matthew, using Mark as a source, edits Mark 6:3 and makes Jesus the son of the *tekton* Joseph. Now if Jesus was a *tekton*, was he poor enough? Though the work of a *tekton* may vary, it is related to some sort of manual work, usually carpentry or masonry. This is not a skilled job that allows Jesus to earn enough income for his family. As John Dominic Crossan suggests, Jesus is more likely "a dispossessed peasant trying to survive as a rural artisan or landless laborer."[17] In other words, he was a marginalized Jew, who was very poor with little means of supporting himself and his family. That is a source of weakness for him.

A more important clue about Jesus' poverty comes from the big picture of the Galilean economy exploited by the elites and Rome. If Jesus was not elite, as the Gospels imply, he simply is one of the poor village people in Nazareth. In ancient Galilee, unlike the modern day techno-business world, opportunities that people can become rich are rare. So the best conjecture is that Jesus lived in poverty like others in the village if he was not a

---

16. See also Matt 13:57; Luke 4:24; John 4:44.

17. Crossan, *Birth of Christianity*, 352; *Historical Jesus*, 421–22. See also Vermes, *Jesus the Jew*.

beggar or social outcast. We do not need a Jesus who is among the poorest to make him a hero of the weak or a champion of liberation. What we see in Jesus is that he experiences poverty like others and struggles with the daily need of clothing and food.

Fifth, the location of Jesus' experience of weakness also has to do with his personality or character. He seems to have an empathizing heart that quickly responds to the need of others. There is no way that we can prove Jesus' personal character, but from inductive reasoning based in the Gospels, it is safe to say that he was a very "emotional" person. For example, Jesus wept (John 11:35; Luke 19:41).[18] While Jesus shares the suffering of others, his weeping also has to do with indignation that he cannot accept the agony of others. What stands out especially is John 11:33: "When Jesus saw her weeping, and the Jews who came with her also weeping, he was greatly *disturbed* in spirit and deeply *moved*." The Greek verbs used here are *brimaomai* and *tarrasso*, respectively, which have more to do with the emotion of "agitation and indignation."[19] So after all, "Jesus wept" (John 11:35). At other times, Jesus' emotion is translated into violent action as seen in the Temple cleansing. Neither is he a passive person who internalizes everything and shuts in himself from the world, nor is he a hasty, impatient, or immature person. Jesus is said to have a balance between emotion and action, knowing when to withdraw and when to move forward. I will come back to this point when we talk about Jesus' weakness in terms of his prayer life.

Jesus' Interpretation of Weakness

Jesus went through various channels of weakness as we have seen so far. He could have lived hopelessly because of all the hostile negative energy induced by weakness—be it personal or spiritual. In fact, during the difficult times of personal and social crises people become hopeless and give up their dreams of a better life. Tears and cries for justice fill the village and yet there still remains deadly silence in Galilee and elsewhere. This is the world

---

18. In general, we can think of several kinds of weeping in the Gospels. Some people weep out of desperate hopelessness (Mark 16:10; Matt 2:18; 5:38; Luke 8:52; 16:10; John 20:11). Others like Peter weep because of their regret (Mark 14:72; Matt 26:75; Luke 22:62). Others weep because of their suffering in punishment (Matt 13:42; 22:13; 24:51; 25:30; Luke 13:28).

19. O'Day, "John," 1931.

that Jesus faces where the mass suffer from all kinds of social maladies and natural disasters. Out of this world and his entangled experience of kinds of weakness, Jesus does not submit to the power of weakness in ways that it dictates him to stay in its darkness without seeing any good in the future. So the option for Jesus is not to sit idle and do nothing without engaging in the world of weakness. With this in mind, we want to know how Jesus responds to such an indefensible power of weakness in his life and in the world. For this task, we will look into Jesus' (re)interpretation of the Spirit, prayer life, water baptism, and religious symbols. Before going there, it would be good to see a wide array of spirit-talk in ancient culture, the Hebrew Bible, and the New Testament. Thus, the following *Excursus* on the Spirit.

Excursus on the Spirit

In order to explore Jesus' relationship with the Spirit, it would be very helpful to put the talk of the spirit into a larger cultural literary context. Once upon a time, primitive people (not in a pejorative sense) thought that the world was full of the spirits. This was the time when people thought that a myriad of spirits manipulated the human world. As time passed, human intellect changed along with cultural or economic changes, and people now think that there must be a hierarchy in the world of gods. Polytheism reflected this belief, according to Greek myths and in other cultures. This view is also found in the Hebrew Bible, before the Davidic monarchy from the tenth century BC to the sixth century BC when monotheism set its roots firmly. Before the Davidic monarchy there were different tribes with their own cultures and gods. But David unified all of the religions and ideologies under the name of Yahweh, making Jerusalem the only cultic place. Eventually, we see an advanced form of human thought in world history around the sixth century BC in the East and West, including ancient Jewish history. The sages thought of the world and religion very differently: The Ultimate Being (personal or not) is responsible for all beings and things in the world. This is the beginning of universalism or monotheistic development in world religions. When it comes to the Hebrew Bible, we see monotheistic development in the so-called Deuteronomistic History. It is not unusual that monotheism goes with monarchy hand in hand. My point about the language of god or the spirit is this: "talk of the spirit is never separated from the talk of god; simply, the spirit is a god, and vice versa." The boundary between god and spirit is blurry; though spirit-talk is further articulated as history progresses. We also should note that spirit-talk is universal in nature throughout the human history. Overall, spirit-talk has the following merits.

1. The spirit-talk is everyday language that people use and feel in their lives. It is not unusual that the Hebrew *ruah* and the Greek *pneuma* mean wind, breath, or the spirit. For example, people can say, "The spirit comes to heal the sick or comfort those who are downtrodden. The spirit imparts her wisdom to us." Many healings in the Hebrew Bible and the New Testament are done through the work of the Spirit, which represents God.

2. The spirit-talk is also helpful to fill in the gap between humanity and God (or the Ultimate). God is invisible, staying transcendently beyond humanity, but the spirit comes to fill in the need of humanity. In this regard, the talk of the spirit is representational. Otherwise, the spirit is hardly a person; it is a way of talking about the work of God.

3. The spirit-talk also has merit because human lives need such talk; otherwise, our lives are boring, hopeless, or aimless. The idea is that we humans are more than what we are and we are more than what we say or feel. As we need a close friend who can talk with us, we need a spirit that advocates for us when we are discouraged or in trouble. We also need a spirit of truth and testimony when we need to speak the truth before the world.

The Spirit in the Bible

Overall, the Spirit is interchangeable with God. As an analogy, if someone says, "My spirit is going with you," it does not mean his or her spirit is a separate person. However, there are a few caveats when we deal with portrayals of the Holy Spirit in the Bible. First, the Bible as a whole does not give us a single view of the Holy Spirit despite some people reading it that way. The Bible has a myriad of traditions about the Spirit: the Spirit's role in creation or in prophetic wisdom tradition, for instance. It is also possible that at times the view of the Spirit is conflicting among different writings. In Acts, Paul says the Spirit leads him to Jerusalem even with all risks, whereas members of his church insist that in their prayer the Holy Spirit does not want him to go to Jerusalem.

Spirit-Talk in the Hebrew Bible

Certainly, we can think of a long process of development of the spirit from Jewish primitive culture down to first-century Judaism under the influence of Hellenism. Like other ancient peoples, Jews before the Davidic monarchy lived in a world of many spirits or gods (polytheism). But as time goes by, they lean toward one god (monotheism) especially after the Babylonian exile experience. So their spiritual talk is advanced to talk about universal wisdom or God's creation. So much so the talk of the spirit is widened and the role of the spirit is diversified: the Spirit as providing wisdom (wisdom literature), as God's representative (prophetic writings), or as God's healing presence (Psalms). There are a variety of forms of the spirit.

"The Spirit of the Lord"

It has to do with anointing David in 1 Sam 16:13 (Isa 61:1); speaking (2 Sam 23:2; Ezek 11:5); as power of the spirit (Ezek 37:1); filled with power (Mic 3:8); as the spirit of wisdom, understanding, counsel and might, and knowledge (Isa 11:2); giving rest (Isa 63:14). See also the following references that use "the spirit of the Lord": Judges 3:10; 6:34; 11:29; 13:25; 14:6, 19; 15:14; 1 Sam 10:6; 16:13f; 2 Sam 23:2; 1 Kings 18:12; 22:24; 2 Kings 2:16; 2 Chr 18:23; 20:14; Isa 11:2; 40:13; 61:1; 63:14; Ezek 11:5; 37:1; Mic 3:8.

"The Spirit of God"

It has to do with prophetic frenzy (1 Sam 19:20); lifting up individuals (Ezek 11:24); as breath of life (Job 27:3; 33:4).

"Holy Spirit"

Ps 51:11; Isa 63:10–11.

"My Spirit"

Gen 6:3; Job 6:4; 7:11; 10:12; 17:1; Ps 31:5; 77:3, 6; 142:3; 143:4, 7; Isa 26:9; 38:16; 42:1; 44:3; 59:21; Ezek 3:14; 36:27; 37:14; 39:29; Dan 2:3; 7:15; Joel 2:28f; Hag 2:5; Zech 4:6; 6:8.

"The Spirit of God"

Gen 41:38; Num 24:2; 1 Sam 10:10; 11:6; 19:20, 23; 2 Chr 15:1; 24:20; Job 27:3; 33:4; Ezek 11:24.

The Spirit in the New Testament

The Spirit works fully through Jesus and other people in the New Testament. We will deal with Jesus' relationship with the Spirit later in this book. So here I will be brief. The Spirit was present before, during, and after Jesus. Even before Jesus, the Spirit was with John the Baptist's birth and worked through other prophets. The Spirit has to do with Jesus at different stages of life: the Spirit's presence with Mary, Jesus' mother; the Spirit's confirmation at his water baptism; Jesus' teaching and healing through the power of the Spirit. We cannot think of Jesus' life or work without talk of the Spirit. In John's Gospel, Jesus embodies the Logos, another name of the Spirit. Upon leaving this world, Jesus prays to the Father for sending a special spirit called the *parakletos* (the Advocate) instead of him (John 14:16, 26; 15:26; 16:7). Jesus understands that the Spirit will replace him after he is gone. At times, in John's Gospel the Spirit has different names: the Spirit of truth (John 14:17; 15:26; 16:13). So the point is that Jesus testifies to the truth (John 18:37) through the Spirit. As Jesus testifies to the truth, his disciples are asked to do the same. That is why Jesus talks about the Spirit of truth in John 14:17; 15:26; and 16:13. The same Spirit of truth was with Jesus and will continue to be with his disciples.

The same Spirit also represents God in heaven. Jesus talks about "spiritual birth" in John 3:1–9. The spiritual birth is none other than a birth from above—the place of God. Of course, the Holy Spirit came to gathered Christians as powerfully as described in Acts 2:1–5 (at Pentecost). Paul also talks about the Spirit without which Christian identity is ineffective or groundless. The Spirit is a source of prayer: "Likewise the Spirit helps us in our *weakness*; for we do not know how to pray as we ought, but that very Spirit intercedes with sighs too deep for words" (Rom 8:26). This point echoes Jesus' prayer life based in weakness that we will explore later. The Spirit is also referred to as "the law of the Spirit of life in Christ Jesus has set you free from the law of sin and of death" (Rom 8:2). Here the law is a principle, so "the law of the Spirit" is the principle of the Spirit and "the law of sin and of death" means the principle of sin and of death. Paul's point is that the Spirit is a driving force and source of Christian life; that is why he puts "of life" to the "law of the Spirit" (so "the law of the Spirit of life"). The Spirit-led life means a death to human selfish will. The opposite is the principle of sin that works through selfish will. Paul's use of the Spirit is very specific for guiding Christian life. Hear what Paul means by the life in the Spirit in Rom 8:6–14:

> To set the mind on the flesh is death, but to set the mind on the Spirit is life and peace. For this reason the mind that is set on the flesh is hostile to God; it does not submit to God's law—indeed it cannot, and those who are in the flesh cannot please God. But you are not in the flesh; you are in the Spirit, since the Spirit of God dwells in you. Anyone who does not have the Spirit of Christ does not belong to him. But if Christ is in you, though the body is dead because of sin, the Spirit is life because of righteousness. If the Spirit of him who raised Jesus from the dead dwells in you, he who raised Christ from the dead will give life to your mortal bodies also through his Spirit that dwells in you. So then, brothers and sisters, we are debtors, not to the flesh, to live according to the flesh—for if you live according to the flesh, you will die; but if by the Spirit you put to death the deeds of the body, you will live. For all who are led by the Spirit of God are children of God.

The Spirit and Jesus

As we have seen in the *Excursus* on the Spirit, the Spirit plays an important role in Jewish tradition. Jesus is led to the Spirit because he is utterly weak and desperately hopeless given the life situation he faces in Galilee.[20] As a Galilean peasant, being landless or a manual worker (*tekton*), Jesus' options are few and so he expresses his utterly broken life experience to the Spirit.[21] During and after Jesus' spiritual experience, what may have happened to him? We can think of several aspects of a change with Jesus. First, his broken spirit is healed through the Spirit. Psalm 51 typifies a Psalmist who

---

20. This view of mine is different from Marcus Borg who believes that Jesus is a Spirit-filled person like ancient Jewish prophets. Borg does not explore how Jesus is led to the Spirit. Basically, he sees Jesus receiving the Spirit. See Borg, *Jesus: A New Vision*, 25–56.

21. Jesus is familiar with the language of the Spirit. He quotes from Isaiah 61 and applies it to himself: "The Spirit of the Lord is upon me, because he has anointed me to bring good news to the poor" (Luke 4:18). Though Borg does not explore Jesus' weakness that leads to the Spirit, his exploration of Jesus' spirituality is a good one. Ibid.

endures a broken spirit: "The sacrifice acceptable to God is *a broken spirit*; a broken and contrite heart, O God, you will not despise." Jesus' spirit breaking comes from two sources: the world's weakness caused by social ills and his own weakness that he cannot deal with the world at once. Through this very act of the spirit breaking he is healed spiritually by the Spirit. Second, because of his healing experience of the spirit, Jesus is supposed to have confidence about him as the son of God. So he rises up against the broken world with his spirit moving forward to mend it. He realizes that human beings are God's creation and that they are supposed to live a good life.

Third, Jesus realizes that the problem of humanity is that people refuse to break their hearts for others. The issue is whether one can participate in the suffering of others through a soft, flexible heart that adequately responds to the world of suffering. Jesus' view is contrasted with that held by society where the unyielding strong people and powers rule the world. While Jesus embraces children, an icon of weakness, he rebukes the fixed minds of adults, an icon of the stubborn people. Jesus advocates for those who are marginalized and weak in society not simply because they are poor or weak but because they are valuable in the eyes of God. Indeed, Jesus' strength/power comes from weakness. Because he is weak, he is strong. That is what Paul perfectly catches a spiritual sense that Jesus means: "Therefore I am content with weaknesses, insults, hardships, persecutions, and calamities for the sake of Christ; for whenever I am weak, then I am strong" (2 Cor 12:10); and "God's weakness is stronger than human strength" (1 Cor 1:25).

Prayers through the Eyes of Weakness

Obviously, Jesus prayed not just once but throughout his life as seen from the Gospel story. Logically speaking, if Jesus had been strong enough to do whatever he wanted, he would not have needed to pray to God. Of course, Jesus' need for prayer is not limited to gaining power. But through prayers, he makes appeals to God and even laments about his situation. At other times, through prayers, he discerns the will of God. In the Gospels there are explicit forms or gesture of prayers by Jesus, and at other times there are unspoken forms of prayers by Jesus. In the following we will look into various forms of Jesus' prayer life.

Prayers for Strength

In order to understand Jesus' prayers for strength, we take Mark 1 as a test case, where Jesus is introduced in a fast paced speed, from Jordan to Galilee to Capernaum.[22] In the middle of his non-stop, hard work in Galilee and Capernaum, he goes to a deserted place to pray: "In the morning, while it was still very dark, he got up and went out to a deserted place, and there he prayed" (Mark 1:35). Jesus needs to reflect on his work and to regain power from the Spirit to continue his work. To see Jesus' need for prayer, we need to see what happened before this time of prayer. In Mark 1, readers are given an overview of his work: 1) Jesus' identity (from Nazareth of Galilee); 2) how he started his ministry (through baptism by John the Baptist); 3) what he did (calling of disciples, teaching about God's rule and healing of the sick); 4) why he did it (for God's rule or God's good news); and 5) how people responded to his work (unprecedented high acclamation). Imagine how quickly Jesus' life moves from one place to another and how tired he may be in dealing with the desperate needs of people. First of all, Jesus goes up to the Jordan to be baptized by John and experiences the Spirit at his baptism. Then he is led to the wilderness to be tested. After the test, Jesus hears about John's arrest and returns to Galilee to do the work of God through proclaiming God's rule and healing the sick. Then he realizes that he cannot do everything by himself and so calls his disciples. Jesus continues to teach about God and cures the sick and casts out the demons. News about Jesus spreads fast throughout the region. People keep coming to Jesus for help and seek him all the time. This is a brief context before he goes to a deserted place for prayer.

From the pace of his ministry, Jesus must have been very tired, physically and spiritually. At this time, his "charged battery" from the Spirit at his water baptism and wilderness test seems to run out and needs recharging. Jesus needs to set aside a special time and place to recharge his spiritual battery by reflecting on his works through the Spirit. At the desert, Jesus checks temptation about his popularity among people and regains the energy necessary for God's good news, which is costly and dangerous because it is not the good news of Rome. In fact, Mark begins with "the good news of Jesus," which is what Jesus lives for. He is not the source of good news, but he brings "the good news of God" to the world (1:14), risking his life.

---

22. A similar case about Jesus' prayer for regaining his strength is found in the story of Jesus' feeding the five thousand (Mark 6:46; Matt 14:23) in that he prays after the great work for similar reasons we identified before.

Surprisingly, the whole Gospel of Mark is framed with good news: the good news of Jesus (1:1) and the good news about Jesus' resurrection (16:8). The challenge from Mark is this: "If women fail to tell the good news about Jesus' work and his resurrection out of their fear that they might be killed, what would you want to do as followers of Jesus?"

Prayers for Healing

From the outset it must be clear that Jesus does not own the power of healing; rather, he becomes a channel of healing for the sick through the Spirit. Because of the urgent need for healing, he does not pray in verbal form. But that does not mean that he did not pray to God for healing. Among the healing stories in the Synoptic Gospels there are three types: healing stories that show the faith of a seeker, healing stories that question the authority of Jesus, and pure healing stories. Examples of each type in the Synoptic Gospels are summarized as follows:

1. Faith-informed healing stories: healing a centurion's servant (Matt 8:5–13; Luke 7:1–10); healing a woman's hemorrhage (Mark 5:25–34; Matt 9:19–22; Luke 8:43–48); restoring sight to two blind men (Matt 9:27–31); healing a Syro-Phoenician woman's daughter (Mark 7:24–30; Matt 15:21–28); and healing a paralytic (Mark 2:1–12; Matt 9:1–8; Luke 5:17–26).

2. Examples of healing stories that question the authority of Jesus: restoring a man's withered hand (Mark 3:1–6; Matt 12:9–14; Luke 6:6–11); and healing a man with dropsy (Luke 14:1–6).

3. Examples of pure healing stories: healing Simon Peter's mother-in-law (Matt 8:14–15; Luke 4:38–39); cleansing a leper (Mark 1:40–45; Matt 8:1–4; Luke 5:12–16); healing a deaf mute (Mark 7:31–37); giving sight to a blind man at Bethsaida (Mark 8:22–26); restoring a woman crippled for eighteen years (Luke 13:10–17); cleansing ten men of leprosy (Luke 17:11–19); and giving sight to a blind man at Jericho (Mark 10:46–52; Matt 20:29–34; Luke 18:35–43).

Among these types of healing miracles, it is in the third type that Jesus clearly engages with the sick and prays with particular words or gestures. So for example, Jesus is "moved with pity" before healing a leper (Mark 1:40–45), which is a form of non-verbal prayer where his action speaks louder than mere words. Before curing a deaf man in Mark 7:31–35, Jesus looks up to heaven, sighs, and says to him: "Be opened (*Ephphatha*)." Here "looking up to heaven" is a mode of prayer in addition to his sigh and word given to the man. Healing does not come from Jesus' own power but from God's power that Jesus unlocks through his prayer that advocates for the weak. Indeed, in this third type the seekers of healing show their desperate needs of restoration. So they approach with words such as "Son of David, have mercy on me" (Mark 10:47–48; Matt 15:22; Luke 18:38–39). We will come back to Jesus' healing in the next chapter.

Prayers of Thanksgiving

Jesus would not need to give thanks to God if he was the owner of his life and if he could do anything that he wished to do. So he thanks God for everything. Jesus finds specific reasons to thank God because God cares for the weak and the marginalized. Such an occasion of thanksgiving is found in Matthew 11:25 (also Luke 10:21): "I thank you, Father, Lord of heaven and earth, because you have hidden these things from the wise and the intelligent and have revealed them to infants." Jesus thanks God because he is the God of the weak (infants), not the God of the wise or the intelligent who seek their own power and wealth at the sacrifice of the weak. On another occasion, Jesus gives thanks to God because he provides for the hungry as well as the poor and dispossessed. Before distributing bread to the five thousand he gives thanks to God (Mark 6:41; Matt 14:19; Luke 9:16; John 6:11).[23] Here again Jesus praises God on behalf of the poor who need daily bread. On still another occasion—at the Last Supper, Jesus gives thanks to God for a cup of wine and a loaf of bread, which seems strange but deeply spiritual (Mark 14:22–23; Matt 26:26–28; Luke 22:17–20). Before his impending peril of death, Jesus acknowledges God's ownership of his life and thanks God for a life of service for him and the world.

Prayers of Petition

At Jesus' farewell discourse in John's Gospel, Jesus gives a long prayer and asks God to sanctify his disciples, who will be left weak since he will be

---

23. Jesus also gives thanks to God in feeding the four thousand (Mark 6:41; Matt 14:19; Luke 9:16; John 6:11).

gone, in the truth (of God) (John 17:17). Earlier, Jesus thanks God for his life for the world. Upon departure from the world, Jesus worries about his disciples and prays to God: "I am not asking you (God) to take them out of the world, but I ask you to protect them from the evil one. They do not belong to the world, just as I do not belong to the world. Sanctify them in the truth; your word is truth. As you have sent me into the world, so I have sent them into the world" (John 17:15–18). Here we see that Jesus makes a petition on behalf of his disciples who will be going through turmoil because of their continual testimony of the truth of God.

Prayers for Discernment

Through his ministry activities Jesus needs to discern God's will. During the early stages of his ministry, Jesus may have thought that his message about God's rule would be well accepted by people. But things did not go in that direction. As the gospel narrative goes on, there are more oppositions coming along the way of his mission journey. At Gethsemane Jesus prays to God to discern God's will (Mark 14:32–39; Matt 26:36–44; Luke 22:41–46; John 18:11). At this juncture of his life Jesus is anguished over the possible threat of his life if he continues his work for God. He certainly struggles with his mission about whether he has to continue or to stop. So he asks God to remove this cup of death if possible, but at the same time he yields to God's will. Even before this dramatic moment at Gethsemane, Jesus frequently seeks God's will. For example, Jesus' prayer during his baptism in the Jordan may be related to discerning God's will that he must carry out in his ministry (Luke 3:21). Before choosing the twelve disciples, Jesus prayed: "Now during those days he went out to the mountain to pray; and he spent the night in prayer to God" (Luke 6:12). Jesus needs wisdom of God before calling the disciples. At other times Jesus teaches his disciples how to pray and what to seek: "Thy will be done on earth as it is in heaven" (Matt 6:10; Luke 11:2).

Prayers of Lament

Jesus laments about his situation on the cross. Jesus says a prayer of lament in Mark 15:34 (also in Matt 27:46): *eli eli lama sabachthani* ("my God, my God, why have you forsaken me?"), which is a quote from Psalm 22.[24] While Luke downplays the difficulties of human suffering, as Jesus asks God to forgive those who are responsible for his crucifixion (Luke 23:34) and entrusts his spirit to God just before his final breath (Luke 23:46), Mark and Matthew do not hide this difficult moment of dying and suffering. Mark and Matthew seem to convey a more realistic picture of the last moment when Jesus prays a prayer of lament. We will come back to this issue in chapter 5 when we deal with a paradoxical event of Jesus' death.

Water Baptism

Mark succinctly and fully describes Jesus' baptism.[25] We can analyze Mark 1:9–11 by looking at five Ws and one H. In v. 9 we read, "In those days" (When) "Jesus came from Nazareth of Galilee" (Who) and "was baptized by John" (What) "in the Jordan" (Where). Then Mark 1:10–11 describes the How and Why of Jesus' baptism: "And just as he was coming up out of the

---

24. Lament psalms deal with difficult human situations and provide engaging spaces to the psalmists when they go through such hard times. See Kim, *Transformative Reading of the Bible*, 48–57.

25. Before exploring Jesus' experience and interpretation of baptism, one thing we should do is establish why the Markan baptism story is closer to the original than Matthew's and Luke's. Scholars have consensus that the Markan version of the baptism story was used as source for Matthew and Luke. This view is based on the so-called Markan Priority. Luke edits the Markan baptism story and removes the details about Jesus' baptism such as the geographical information (Nazareth, Jordan) or the agent information (John). Instead, Luke emphasizes Jesus' prayer along with people's presence with him. The reason for omitting such information may have to do with Luke's interest in making the gospel more universal because of its primary audience of the Gentiles. Or, it is also possible that Luke hides the fact that Jesus was baptized by John because Jesus is supposed to be more authoritative than John. Now Matthew significantly changes the source material in Mark. Here John hesitates to baptize Jesus, but Jesus asks him to do so and explains why such a baptism is necessary for fulfilling the righteousness. This change is understandable from the perspective of Jewish audience for whom the righteousness is a very crucial theological topic. At any rate, Matthew deals with the need of Jesus' baptism by John, which implies that some members in the Matthean community may have felt uncomfortable with Jesus' baptism by John, perhaps for two understandable reasons: 1) a matter of who is higher in terms of authority; 2) the fact that John's baptism is that of repentance for the forgiveness of sins (Mark 1:4–5). Perhaps this kind of the Matthean situation requires Matthew to retell the baptism story and convinces his audience to believe that Jesus' baptism is not a matter of authority or sins but a matter of fulfilling the righteousness. The bottom line is that the Markan baptism story, though short, is most fully explored without omitting any information unlike Matthew or Luke. This is why we analyze Markan baptism story here.

water, he saw the heavens torn apart and the Spirit descending like a dove on him. And a voice came from heaven, 'You are my Son, the Beloved; with you I am well pleased.'" Based on this Markan baptism story, we will see in detail how Jesus re-ritualizes his baptism in view of his response to the "weakness" that surrounds him and the world.

In Those Days (When)

Jesus comes to the Jordan during a particular time ("in those days") (Mark 1:9), when Israel is in despair and its people suffer from poverty, oppression, and exploitation by the powers in Jerusalem and Rome. From this we can infer that the timing of Jesus' baptism is not randomly chosen by him, but carefully decided to occur during a critical time that he is called to serve his people. "In those days" refers not only to a narrative transition from one scene to another but to the time of Jesus' life in first-century Galilee under control of Rome. "In those days" Jesus comes from Nazareth of Galilee, which is a very outdated isolated town near Sepphoris and distant from Jerusalem. Galilean peasants scream for justice and rise up against the harsh inhumane unjust rule by Rome and local elites. Their God is taught in one way, but he is not really practiced in everyday life in Galilee and elsewhere. Jesus himself is one of the peasants or manual workers (*tekton*) who experience all kinds of weakness in his village. In a way, he himself was poor and at the brink of dying. At this desperate life stage in a local village Jesus wonders if God is alive and why all these bad things happen. He finds dissonance between God's rule and the reality in the world.

John the Baptist also rises in this context where God's rule must be restored. He is very critical of the current leaders of Palestine and asks them to repent. Many people—except for the most socially elite—come to the Jordan to be baptized and renewed. Jesus hears about this work of John the Baptist and decides to go see him and is baptized by him. This is the historical context of Jesus' baptism: "In those days Jesus came from Nazareth of Galilee."

In the Jordan (Where)

The place of the Jordan is significant since people come to be baptized by John. Jesus comes to the Jordan where John the Baptist baptizes people for their renewal for a new kingdom of God. The Jordan is on the edge of wilderness, and thus it "represents a long journey of Israelites after the exodus because they did not follow God's will (Num 14:33–34; 32:13)."[26] The Jordan River is a symbolic place of testing and faith through which Israelites enter a new land of promise (Josh 3:1—4:24).

Baptized In the Water (How)

Jesus enters the Jordan River to be baptized. This act of entering the water symbolizes or signifies a few things: 1) surrender to God; 2) denial of the self; and 3) new birth or renewal. First, surrender to God means an attitude of "I am small before you." Second, likewise, entering into the water means death of the self. Following John's lead on baptism, Jesus allows his body to be pulled up by John. Third, new birth or renewal means a renewed identity through death of the self. The self that dies for Jesus may be his despair about the world, lack of trust in God, and passivism.[27] What is renewing in him is the opposite of this: his commitment to God's work. His new identity begins with water (a place of death) and not through fire (an image of the Spirit at the Pentecost in Acts 2).[28]

Reborn as the Beloved Son of God (Why)

A voice from heaven confirms that Jesus is the beloved son of God, who is strong now through submitting to God. As a result of all this dying-and-rising experience, Jesus is re-birthed as the Son of God. The heavenly voice says that Jesus is the beloved son of God, who will do God's work.[29] This

---

26. Kim, *Resurrecting Jesus*.

27. My reading of Jesus' baptism is very different from a traditional one, as is seen in the Book of Order W.2.3000 in the Presbyterian Church (USA): "Baptism is the sign and seal of incorporation into Christ. Jesus through his own baptism identified himself with sinners in order to fulfill all righteousness. Jesus in his own baptism was attested Son by the Father and was anointed with the Holy Spirit to undertake the way of the servant manifested in his sufferings, death and resurrection." The above traditional interpretation about Jesus' baptism loses the plausible existential experience of Jesus' baptism: dying and renewal. Instead, what is emphasized here is that Jesus merely identified with the weak, and the implication is that he himself was not weak.

28. The main symbol of baptism is water, and the Holy Spirit comes as a result of the baptism.

29. The heavenly voice is a spiritual one that cannot be heard by other people than the one who is called and experiences a moment of Spirit descending. So we do not know what has really happened to Jesus at his baptism. Albert Schweitzer thinks that Jesus'

special experience of Jesus can be understood as a call narrative. Otherwise, this event should not be understood as a unique special event that gives Jesus once-and-forever power. Davies argues that Jesus' baptism is a watershed event by which Jesus is possessed by the Spirit and becomes a charismatic healer.[30] He is touched by the Spirit and called "my son, the beloved!" What else does he need? He is no longer fatherless in the world where many are lost.

Religious Symbols

Jesus reinterprets religious symbols with a focus on caring for the weak. For the Pharisees, the law is a collection of commandments that must be kept without exceptions. However, for Jesus it is a symbol of God's mercy and justice through which God's creation is equally protected and blessed. It is believed that Jesus has a different notion of law as a "principle" that people have to follow. While the Hebrew *torah* is typically translated as law, its plain meaning is "teaching or instruction." For example, parents teach their children the "torah." The Psalmist also refers to God's teaching: "Blessed are those who do not follow the advice of the wicked . . . but their delight is in the *torah* of the Lord, and on his *torah* they meditate day and night" (Ps 1:1–2). Here "torah" does not refer to the five books of Moses called the Torah in Judaism or to particular law codes such as the covenant code in Exodus 20:19 and 23:33.[31] With this plain sense of law as "teaching or instruction," it is inferred that Jesus understands God's torah as God's primary teaching that people have to follow: that is a mind of mercy and justice. Because of this understanding, Jesus expects that the sick should be healed even on the Sabbath and even enemies can be loved.

Jesus also reinterprets the temple as a place of renewal and thanksgiving. In Jesus' time the temple did not function well. It became the center of elite power and politics. Jesus' act of cleansing the temple can be understood from this perspective. Jesus cannot stay quiet upon seeing money changers and sellers of sacrifice animals because the temple is more than a place, but a symbol of God's presence through which the weak and marginalized are protected and renewed in times of crisis.

---

baptism experience is hallucination. See Schweitzer, *Psychiatric Study of Jesus*, 72.

30. Davies, *Jesus the Healer*, 104.

31. Even the Greek *nomos* connotes "principle" as well as "law."

Third, Jesus also reinterprets the Sabbath through the spirit of God's law, which is mercy and justice. Caring for the sick and the poor cannot stop on the Sabbath. That is why Jesus rebuts the Pharisees' accusation about the breaking of the Sabbath, saying "The sabbath was made for humankind, and not humankind for the sabbath" (Mark 2:27).[32] The Sabbath is a day of celebration of God's creation. If there are some people left out in that celebration, the Sabbath would be incomplete. In this sense, the Sabbath did not come to many people in Jesus' time. Jesus actively engages in restoring God's creation by teaching about God's rule and healing the sick.

Summary

Jesus himself was marginalized and subjected to discriminatory shame because of his low family background and social status. An alternative virtue is to break mind and heart before God and the world. So Jesus advocates an alternative wisdom of weakness that challenges a dominant system based on power. While the mainline society says that the strong rule the world, Jesus offers a different view that the world must be ruled by mercy and solidarity. The next chapter is about Jesus' work through the eyes of weakness.

---

32. Banks, *Jesus and the Law*, 125–72.

5

Jesus' Enactment of Weakness

THROUGH THE EYES OF weakness Jesus not only sees the world but enacts "weakness" for the kingdom of God (as God's rule here and now). Jesus reimagines the world through teaching in parables, challenges the status quo, and advocates for the weak. In this chapter we will see how Jesus enacts his interpretation of weakness in his teaching and ministry. The select parables of Jesus will be explored in view of the following three points: 1) how weakness is understood and related to God's rule; 2) what challenge there is for the reader; and 3) what Jesus imagines to be an ideal state of God's rule. Overall, through parables Jesus emphasizes the importance of mercy in the rule of God.[1] Jesus says: "I desire mercy and not sacrifice" (Matt 12:7, quote from Hosea 6:6).[2] Mercy comes even before tradition or law, as Jesus reinterprets the Sabbath law (Mark 2:27). Mercy is a mind of weakness that has compassion for the poor and the marginalized.[3] People who receive God's mercy have to show their mercy toward others. In order to teach about the centrality of mercy in God's rule Jesus tells many parables through which he challenges those hardened hearts to accept an alternative world based on weakness-informed virtue.

---

1. God's rule is the content of "the good news of God" that Jesus proclaims (Mark 1:14). "The good news of God" means either "the good news about God" or "God becoming the good news." In whichever sense, Jesus tells people that God, not the Roman emperor or any human masters, is the good news because God is merciful and just.

2. See also Mark 2:17; 12:33; Matt 9:13; Luke 5:31–32.

3. This kind of God who has compassion for the socially marginalized such the widows, orphans, the poor, and aliens are well preserved in Deut 10:17–19. For more, see Wafawanaka, *Am I Still My Brother's Keeper?*

In addition to the parables of Jesus, his social activism—such as temple cleansing—shows his weakness-informed, heart-aching solidarity with the weak. That is, Jesus' heart breaks and he cannot watch money changers when the temple does not function for the weak. Through this social action, he challenges the strong and embraces the weak. Lastly, Jesus' healing miracles will be explored in view of his lens of weakness. Undoubtedly, here Jesus is found fully engaged with the sick.

Teaching in Parables

Mustard Seed (Mark 4:30–32; Matt 13:31–32; Luke 13:18–19; Thom 20)

> He also said, "With what can we compare the kingdom of God, or what parable will we use for it? It is like a mustard seed, which, when sown upon the ground, is the smallest of all the seeds on earth; yet when it is sown it grows up and becomes the greatest of all shrubs, and puts forth large branches, so that the birds of the air can make nests in its shade." (Mark 4:30–32)

Through the Eyes of Weakness

In consideration of the dominant culture in Jesus' time that seeks power and greatness, Jesus' choice of the mustard seed in this parable is untraditional, challenging, and subversive. The idea of a "mustard seed" parable is new and striking to his hearers. Normally, God's rule would be compared to a cedar tree in Jewish tradition as in Ezek 17:22–23:

> Thus says the Lord GOD: I myself will take a sprig from the lofty top of a cedar; I will set it out. I will break off a tender one from the topmost of its young twigs; I myself will plant it on a high and lofty mountain. On the mountain height of Israel I will plant it, in order that it may produce boughs and bear fruit, and become a noble cedar. Under it every kind of bird will live; in the shade of its branches will nest winged creatures of every kind.

A cedar tree grows on the high snowy mountains in Lebanon, two thousand meters from the sea level. It stands forty meters high, with a diameter of three meters and lifespan of two to three thousand years. The cedar tree, appearing seventy times in the Hebrew Bible, is deluxe wood material used for palaces (Ps 104:16) and represents glory (Isa 35:2, 60:13); power (Ps 29:5); magnificence (1 Kings 19:23; Isa 2:13); and authority (1 Kings 4:33; 2 Kings 14:9; Zech 11:1).

As we see here, the hearers' usual expectations about God's rule would likely come from a metaphor of greatness that is represented by a cedar tree. But Jesus uses a mustard seed to refer to God's rule. A mustard seed is a symbol of smallness or of a trivial thing. Regarding the size of the mustard seed, the gospel texts do not describe it in the same way. In Mark, the seed is "the smallest of all the seeds on earth," and in Matthew it is "the smallest of all the seeds." However, Luke does not talk about its size. Scientifically speaking, the mustard seed is not the smallest seed on earth or the smallest seed of all the seeds. While we do not know exactly what Jesus' original words are in this parable, the Evangelists' agree that the mustard seed represents something small. The important thing is not whether this seed is really the smallest on earth or among all the seeds because the parable is not about horticulture or science.

Challenge to the Reader

Jesus challenges the culture of the cedar tree in his time and those who seek great things such as power and wealth while looking down upon the weak and socially vulnerable. He does not say that God's rule is like a cedar tree. People must know that everything begins small, and each is beautiful on its own. This parable challenges the culture of competition and that of seeking to be great. Jesus points out that a small mustard seed grows big enough to serve others by providing shade for birds and humans. People think that the mustard seed or plant is trivial compared to a cedar tree, but Jesus says that a small seed grows into a tree on which birds of the air can make nests. The three Evangelists do not exactly agree on the details about the growth of the mustard seed. According to Mark, it "becomes the greatest of all shrubs, and puts forth large branches, so that the birds of the air can make nests in its shade" (Mark 4:32); while Matthew states that "it is the greatest of shrubs and becomes a tree, so that the birds of the air come and make nests in its branches" (Matt 13:32). But Luke says: "It grew and became a tree, and the birds of the air made nests in its branches" (Luke 13:19). Mark's description is realistic as we observe in nature that the mustard seed does not grow into an actual tree. From a perspective of arboreal science, the mustard plant is not a tree. But from the perspective of two of the evangelists, it is a tree. According to Mark, it puts forth large branches so that the birds of the air can make nests in its shade. The branches of the mustard plants are strong enough and its shade is good enough for the birds of the air. Matthew and Luke are right in saying that the mustard seed becomes a tree, in that it serves many of the same purposes of a tree. The mustard plant is strong enough and serves the birds of the air and people who need it for food or medicine. Even though it is not a tallest tree in the world, the mustard plant is a beautiful plant in its own right. So the challenge for powerful people is that they are not the only powerful trees or branches. Birds can sit on the mustard plants too. Jesus challenges them not to boast about the size of wealth or power. Rather, the point is how to serve others.

An Ideal State of God's Rule

A beautiful world that Jesus re-imagines is not only of the strong or of the weak. There are lofty cedar trees on high mountains and there are also everyday plants or trees like mustard plants. Both cedar trees and mustard plants are a part of God's creation. But the issue for humanity is what we think about them and how we can use them for God's rule. That is, the cedar trees have to be used for building houses for everyday people, not for the strong only. Furthermore, the mustard plants are not to be looked down upon or judged as being harmful. In everyday life they are helpful for food or medicinal purposes. They are also very useful for the birds of the air. They are plentiful and can be accessed easily by many ordinary people. In society some people are treated as nothing or harmful and thus are looked down upon. But in God's rule they can become useful if their usefulness is found and used in the right place. That is why Jesus eats and talks with tax-collectors or other kinds of sinners in society. They have potential that can be used beautifully in God's rule. In order to build such a world of God's rule, people have to be cultivated to embrace the importance of smallness. While people aim to be cedar trees, Jesus asks them to be like a mustard seed, which can grow big enough to give service to birds and people. People need a new lens to see that small and weak people in society have potential and that they are beautiful.

Leaven (Matt 13:33b; Luke 13:20b–21; Thom 96)

> The kingdom of heaven is like leaven that a woman took and hid in three measures of flour until all of it was leavened. (Matt 13:33)

Through the Eyes of Weakness

The parable about leaven is considered one of the most authentic parables of Jesus because of its content. Jesus introduces a subversive story about God's rule (*basileia tou theou*) by relating it to leaven. Scholars believe that this parable of the leaven must be authentic to Jesus because it is unconventional and striking to the extent that leaven is almost always used negatively in public discourse. It represents something or someone who corrupts other things or people.[4] The source of this metaphor comes from the image of a swollen corpse in the streets. However, using leaven as a metaphorical substance in the parable, Jesus reverses the hearers' expectation about leaven. That is, leaven is small and hidden, but it does marvelously great things. Leaven makes bread tasty. Families can gather around the bread table and enjoy fellowship with one another. As we saw in the mustard seed parable, Jesus seems to teach that one should become humble to serve others. Jesus seems to say, "Be leaven; be small and do not show off what you have. If you are a good person from society's perspective, know that you are small and serve the community without revealing your identity. If you are judged as a bad or weak person, know that God can use you too."

The woman's work in this parable is also striking. Leaven alone is not enough because it should be taken by somebody and placed in the right place. In this case, this somebody is a woman, who recognizes the greatness of small leaven and takes and hides it in the right place. This woman is like a great agent of God. She does everything from taking leaven, to mixing flour, to making bread. In that society, woman is considered weak and her work is treated as being trivial, but in God's rule a woman that attends to smallness and takes care of it is a model to follow.

---

4. For example, see what Jesus says in Mark 8:15; Matt 16:6; and Luke 12:1. Even Paul uses leaven negatively in 1 Cor 5:6–8.

Challenge to the Reader

Through this parable, Jesus challenges those who have a fixed mind and do not see the hidden, small, yet powerful element of leaven in the process of bread making. They cannot see such an important function of leaven because they have a fixed idea that every good thing is noticeable due to its splendor, just like a cedar tree in the mustard seed parable. What is worse is that people already have prejudices about leaven, which is viewed as a source of evil or corruption. It is true that even Jesus and Paul use leaven as a negative metaphor. Except for this parable, Jesus uses leaven as a negative metaphor and asks his disciples to be careful about the Pharisees' leaven (Mark 8:15; Matt 16:6; Luke 12:1). Similarly, Paul also warns against leaven in his response to various congregations: "A little yeast leavens the whole batch of dough" (Gal 5:9); "Your boasting is not a good thing. Do you not know that a little yeast leavens the whole batch of dough? Clean out the old yeast so that you may be a new batch, as you really are unleavened. For our paschal lamb, Christ, has been sacrificed. Therefore, let us celebrate the festival, not with the old yeast, the yeast of malice and evil, but with the unleavened bread of sincerity and truth" (1 Cor 5:6–8).

This negative use of leaven is one possible use in context. However, in this parable, Jesus twists the use of such a fixed cultural metaphor and shifts it to have a new positive meaning that is important to God's rule. In addition to the importance of a small element in God's rule, like a mustard seed, Jesus sees the importance of hidden service. So his challenge to his readers is that they work hard without wanting to receive much in return. In fact, leaven is used for benefiting others (tasty bread and people who eat it), not for itself. We also should know that the woman plays a great role in the parable because she recognizes the value of leaven and places it in the right place. So here the challenge is that society or community needs to recognize the value of leaven-like people or anyone who seems trivial in the eyes of society and to give them an opportunity to serve in the community. In view of a male dominant society, the woman's active role here should be a great challenge to those males.

An Ideal State of God's Rule

An ideal world that Jesus seems to re-imagine is not only of the males or of the females. In this time when Jesus tells this parable, most people are engaged in farming. Most males work in the field and return home for rest and dinner. In homes women prepare food and bread for the family. In such a traditional community, each person must have a place and role. There should not be a gender hierarchy that men are more important than women or that women's work is secondary. At a dinner table, family members gather around to eat bread in fellowship. To enjoy truly such a peaceful union, there must be hard work from all members, inside and outside of the home, whether their work is noticeable or not. Life together means a life of service in each member's place.

Vineyard Laborers and Employer (Matt 20:1–16)

> For the kingdom of heaven is like a landowner who went out early in the morning to hire laborers for his vineyard. After agreeing with the laborers for the usual daily wage, he sent them into his vineyard. When he went out about nine o'clock, he saw others standing idle in the marketplace; and he said to them, "You also go into the vineyard, and I will pay you what is right." So they went. When he went out again about noon and about three o'clock, he did the same. And about five o'clock he went out and found others standing around; and he said to them, "Why are you standing here idle all day?" They said to him, "Because no one has hired us." He said to them, "You also go into the vineyard." When evening came, the owner of the vineyard said to his manager, "Call the laborers and give them their pay, beginning with the last and then going to the first." When those hired about five o'clock came, each of them received the usual daily wage. Now when the first came, they thought they would receive more; but each of them also received the usual daily wage. And when they received it, they grumbled against the landowner, saying, "These last worked only one hour, and you have made them equal to us who have borne the burden of the day and the scorching heat." But he replied to one of them, "Friend, I am doing you no wrong; did you not agree with me for the usual daily wage? Take what belongs to you and go; I choose to give to this last the same as I give to you. Am I not allowed to do what I choose with what belongs to me? Or are you envious because I am generous?" So the last will be first, and the first will be last.

Through the Eyes of Weakness

From God's perspective all families on earth should be fed enough and taken care of because they are God's creation. But in the real world the weak and the marginalized are at the mercy of the strong, who exploit them in order to maximize their profits. Likewise, their concern is not to employ all who need work but to maintain a patron-client system. In this regard, this parable is about economic justice and full employment. Unlike the masters in society who abuse and exploit their workers, the master in this story does more than expected when caring for the needy. He goes out to the labor market five times. This is unusual and perhaps impractical because since the master knows how many workers he needs for the vineyard, he could have hired all that he needed at once. Or he may have not found enough workers each time he went out. At any rate, what we hear from this story is that going out five times to seek workers is unusual and may imply his strong intention to give jobs to all. In other words, he may have been interested in hiring all in the market (we call it "full employment"). So the master sends all workers into his vineyard at different times, which means not all worked for the same hours. But in the end the master pays all the same as he intended and promised to them.

Challenge to the Reader

When it comes time to pay, the master gives all employed the same wage of one denarion—the usual daily wage—regardless of how much they worked.[5] So the "early birds" complained to him, but the master defends his action in two ways. One is about legal matters; that is to say, his point is that he did not do anything wrong because he paid the promised wage of one denarion (the usual daily wage) to them.[6] The other is about his character, as the master says: "Am I not allowed to do what I choose with what belongs to me? Or are you envious because I am *good*?" (20:15). Here

---

5. The parable is clear about the reason for them not being hired early enough; it is not because of their laziness but because of no employers wanting to hire them: "Because no one has hired us" (Matt 20:7).

6. Some scholars see the master in the parable negatively as an abusive, arrogant master who in the end does not pay enough to all, while feeding the spirit of competition. Herzog, *Parables as Subversive Speech*, 94–96. See Buttrick, *Speaking Parables*, 114. But this negative reading may not seem so strong because the master is concerned with full employment and adequate pay to all his workers.

"good" (*agathos* in Greek) is the character of God. In other words, the point is not that God is all powerful or generous but that God is good. God is good because he wants to give "what is just or right" (*ho dikaios*, Matt 20:4) to all workers.[7] Overall, Jesus' point is that people need to show mercy and solidarity with others by sharing what they have. The problem with "early birds" is that they do not evidence a merciful or "broken" spirit attuned to the brokenness of other people's lives. Jesus' further challenge to his audience and society is that the employers (masters) in society have to imitate God's mercy and justice. The primary point of God's character that Jesus emphasizes is not the power of God by which God can do anything but his mercy that he extends to all, especially the poor and the marginalized. The weak should be restored by being provided work and pay, not because they are poor, but because they are God's creation.

An Ideal State of God's Rule

The vineyard is a metaphor that points to various things: employment, community, society, nation, or even the global community (the world as God's vineyard). As humans are imperfect and vulnerable to various adverse life conditions such as sickness or family emergency, it is impossible that all are equally capable to work. That is what the marketplace in this parable depicts: some came early and were picked up by the employer, and some others were left not employed because they were not sought out by any employer. They were looking for jobs, but somehow they were less capable for unknown reasons. But the bottom line is that all people need a job. A society that can accept the weak as part of the community and give them an opportunity to work with their capacities seems close to an ideal world. So people in an ideal world could and should ask others: Did you eat? This type of question was actually a greeting that I heard and said a lot while I growing up in a Korean farming village. The point of this greeting is to make sure that all are fed enough on particular days. Checking the need of others is the starting point in God's rule.

---

7. Levine, *Short Stories by Jesus*, 217–18.

Lost Sheep (Matt 18:12–14; Luke 15:3–7; Thom 107)

What do you think? If a shepherd has a hundred sheep, and one of them has gone astray, does he not leave the ninety-nine on the mountains and go in search of the one that went astray? And if he finds it, truly I tell you, he rejoices over it more than over the ninety-nine that never went astray. *So it is not the will of your Father in heaven that one of these little ones should be lost.* (Matt 18:12–14; italics are mine and indicate that these are the Evangelist's redaction)

So he told them this parable: "Which one of you, having a hundred sheep and losing one of them, does not leave the ninety-nine in the wilderness and go after the one that is lost until he finds it? When he has found it, he lays it on his shoulders and rejoices. And when he comes home, he calls together his friends and neighbors, saying to them, "Rejoice with me, for I have found my sheep that was lost." *Just so, I tell you, there will be more joy in heaven over one sinner who repents than over ninety-nine righteous persons who need no repentance.* (Luke 15:3–7; italics are mine and indicate that these are the Evangelist's redaction)

Jesus said, The kingdom is like a shepherd who had a hundred sheep. One of them, the largest, went astray. He left the ninety-nine and looked for the one until he found it. After he had toiled, he said to the sheep, "I love you more than the ninety-nine." Gos. Thom 107

Through the Eyes of Weakness

Perhaps societycould say it is logical that one can be lost for the sake of one hundred. Especially in a dangerous situation in which costs are significant, the leader of the community may want to sacrifice one member and give up searching. Likewise, in this parable one lost sheep can be abandoned and a shepherd can go on with the rest. Such a response may seem normal to many. The original parable of Jesus underwent significant changes in its transmission by word or letter. If we take out all possible redactional elements from Luke and Matthew, we can get closer to the early form of the lost sheep parable told by Jesus.[8] In that plausible version the parable

---

8. While the Evangelists edit the original parable of the lost sheep to fit in their

goes like this: "One day, a shepherd had a hundred sheep and lost one. Then leaving the ninety-nine, will he not go out to search for one lost or wandering sheep? With every effort made, if a sheep is found, how much he will rejoice?"

Through the eyes of weakness, one out of one hundred is not just a number, but a real life being lost. Nobody can be insignificant to anyone. This parable of the lost sheep is a counter-balance to a culture such as that in Jesus' time where social outcasts and the weak are left out and neglected.

Challenge to the Reader

With this simple version of the parable, first of all, Jesus teaches that God's rule must include the weak or the lost, even one out of a hundred members. In God's rule, not a single person can be left out or ignored. This does not mean that the ninety-nine can be sacrificed for just one. Some scholars have hard time understanding the shepherd's action of leaving the ninety-nine to search for just one sheep. Reasonably speaking, the wise shepherd would not abandon the ninety-nine sheep unattended to seek just one. So the logical guess from this story is that he probably first secured a place of protection for the ninety-nine in the wilderness or asked one of his workers to take care of them. After that, he would leave for the lost. The point is therefore that the shepherd cannot give up the one lost sheep because the one is insignificant.

Second, Jesus highlights a leader's qualifications or attitude about the weak members in God's rule. Like the shepherd who immediately senses the loss of one sheep, the desirable leader must have that same sense about his/her members. In other words, what is required for the shepherd/leader is a sense of mercy or solidarity with the weak members. Without that sense

---

theological contexts, Jesus' original parable would likely have been simple and clear without having details about the meaning. For example, Luke connects the lost sheep with the lost sinner who repents and returns to the sheepfold. But this added allegorical interpretation by Luke is funny because the lost sheep cannot repent. More than that, the focus in the parable proper is not the lost sheep that returns but the shepherd who makes every effort to find it. It is understandable, however, why Luke interprets this parable that way; it is because the Lucan community has to tell his largely Gentile audience that the only condition for joining the beloved community is to repent and return. On the other hand, Matthew interprets this parable with a focus on the marginalized, "one of the least of these" (Matt 25:40, 45). All these theological issues in Matthew and Luke are responsible for the current, changed versions of the parable.

the leader/shepherd would never even recognize the absence or loss of the one weak member.

An Ideal State of God's Rule

An ideal world conceived by Jesus is that all are under the care of the responsible leader. To make this happen, not only the leader but members of the community should know what is happening to others. Sometimes the issue is that people are so caught up with their own lives that do not know what is happening to others. As seen in the parable, the shepherd could go on herding without knowing that he had lost a sheep. The leader or members of the community must have an ability to empathize with the lost one because from the perspective of the lost one, he lost the world of familiarity and security.

Samaritan (Luke 10:30b–37)

> Jesus replied, "A man was going down from Jerusalem to Jericho, and fell into the hands of robbers, who stripped him, beat him, and went away, leaving him half dead. Now by chance a priest was going down that road; and when he saw him, he passed by on the other side. So likewise a Levite, when he came to the place and saw him, passed by on the other side. But a Samaritan while traveling came near him; and when he saw him, he was moved with pity. He went to him and bandaged his wounds, having poured oil and wine on them. Then he put him on his own animal, brought him to an inn, and took care of him. The next day he took out two denarii, gave them to the innkeeper, and said, 'Take care of him; and when I come back, I will repay you whatever more you spend.' Which of these three, do you think, was a neighbor to the man who fell into the hands of the robbers?" He said, "The one who showed him mercy." Jesus said to him, "Go and do likewise." Luke 10:30–37

Through the Eyes of Weakness

The parable of the Good Samaritan has been typically read as a moral story that exemplifies the importance of helping the victim or the marginalized. But we cannot stop here because Jesus' parable is a subversive story that challenges hearers' familiar thoughts on certain customs. For Jews neighbors are friends or relatives, but the Samaritans are never their neighbors. There is a clear boundary between "us" and "them." In this context, one of the critical issues raised in this parable is the concept of neighbor. With a triadic formula story, three individuals pass by a victim. The first one is a priest, the second one is a Levite, and both of them pass by without stopping to care for the victim. The third one, a Samaritan, is not a fellow Jew and therefore is not bound to help the victim. But he stops when he gets to him and does everything he can to help him. From the hearers' perspective, this newly introduced third man being a Samaritan would be a total shock. On the one hand, their religious leaders were supposed to help a fellow victim; and on the other hand, the last helping hand is not one of their fellow Jews but a person from an enemy region.

At the end of the story, Jesus asks the lawyer: Who is a neighbor to a person in need? The answer is the person who showed mercy. The lawyer's original definition of neighbor loses footing now, because according to this story and Jesus' question, a neighbor is someone who shows mercy, not someone who receives mercy. Jesus' point must be something like this: "You are to be a neighbor to others; do not look for your familiar neighbors out there to see who deserves your care or love. In doing so, go beyond race or physical appearance. Just stop there and have mercy and do what you can." Jesus tells this parable by redefining who is neighbor and thus challenges those who practice a dsicriminating charity or love. The weak or the marginalized can be seen and cared for by those with a changed view of neighbor.

The Challenge to the Reader

The problem for the priest and Levite is a lack of mercy. Their hearts were hardened and therefore they could not respond to the need of the victim at such a critical moment. Otherwise, there are no legitimate excuses made by the priest or the Levite on the basis of religious duty. Jewish laws allow for a priest to do necessary things in emergency situations like this. For example, he could bury the corpse if he was dead. To do so, he should have approached the victim to find what was going on. Still, since he was going down to Jericho, he was not on the way to Temple duty. So the problem is his simple lack of compassion or mercy. His heart was not responsive to the suffering of others.

An Ideal State of God's Rule

In contrast, the Samaritan man focused on the victim's situation, nothing more or nothing less. He had mercy toward the victim. He did not care whether the victim was a Jew or a woman or a child. His heart was moved and his body ached because he had mercy and compassion. This person is ideal in God's rule because he has a heart that breaks because of the suffering of others. In fact, the victim in this parable is also a beautiful child of God who needs recovery of strength through proper care. Jesus proclaims that God's rule has come, but in reality there are still people left unattended and abandoned.

Unmerciful Servant (Matt 18:23–35)

> "For this reason the kingdom of heaven may be compared to a king who wished to settle accounts with his slaves. When he began the reckoning, one who owed him ten thousand talents was brought to him; and, as he could not pay, his lord ordered him to be sold, together with his wife and children and all his possessions, and payment to be made. So the slave fell on his knees before him, saying, 'Have patience with me, and I will pay you everything.' And out of pity for him, the lord of that slave released him and forgave him the debt. But that same slave, as he went out, came upon one of his fellow slaves who owed him a hundred denarii; and seizing him by the throat, he said, 'Pay what you owe.' Then his fellow slave fell down and pleaded with him, 'Have patience with me, and I will pay you.' But he refused; then he went and threw him into prison until he would pay the debt. When his fellow slaves saw what had happened, they were greatly distressed, and they went and reported to their lord all that had taken place. Then his lord summoned him and said to him, 'You wicked slave! I forgave you all that debt because you pleaded with me. Should you not have had mercy on your fellow slave, as I had mercy on you?' *And in anger his lord handed him over to be tortured until he would pay his entire debt. So my heavenly Father will also do to every one of you, if you do not forgive your brother or sister from your heart."*
> Matt 18:23–35

Through the Eyes of Weakness

Like other parables in Matthew, this parable also undergoes editorial changes by the Evangleist to fit into his theological context where God's limitless forgiveness is a starting point for the community. We should, therefore, reconstruct the would-be original parable of Jesus from which our interpretation will come. Matthew retells and interprets Jesus' parable allegorically, changing the master (*kyrios*) to king (*basileius*) in verse 23, which implies God in Matthew, and perhaps changing the debt of 10,000 denarii to 10,000 talents to indicate an incalculable amount of money that can be forgiven.[9] If we remove the possible editorial changes, we will have an approximate version of the original—the pre-Matthean form of the parable. The following is such a form suggested by Martinus de Boer:[10]

> A person wished to settle accounts with his servants. After he had begun reckoning, one debtor of 10,000 denarii was brought to him. And because he was unable to pay up, the master commanded him to be sold, with his wife and children and all that he had, and the sum to be repaid. So the servant fell down and was beseeching him, saying, "Be patient with me, and I shall repay you everything." And the master of that servant was moved to pity and released him and forgave him the loan.

That servant went out and found one of his fellow servants, who owed him one hundred denarii, and he grabbed and choked him, saying, "Pay up what you owe." So his fellow servant fell down and was beseeching him, saying, "Be patient with me, and I shall repay you." He did not wish to do so, but went and threw him into prison, until he should pay what was owed.

When his fellow servants saw what had happened, they were greatly shocked and went and reported to their master all that had happened. Then his master summoned him and said to him, "Evil servant, I forgave you all that debt, since you beseeched me. Was it not necessary also for you to have had mercy on your fellow servant, as I had mercy on you?" And his master

---

9. But ironically, Matthew's intention about a forgiving God is not very successful because this master eventually punishes the forgiven slave. At any rate, Matthew's point is that there is an end of the world and until then God's mercy will be available. Verses 34–35 are apparently Matthew's comments about the meaning of the parable, which is Matthew's consistent theology about future judgment and interim ethics.

10. See de Boer, "Ten Thousand Talents," 230. See also Crossan, *In Parables*, 108; Scott, "King's Accounting," 433–34.

became angry and handed him over to the jailers until he should pay up all what was owed.

Based on the above reconstructed version, Jesus teaches the centrality of mercy toward others in God's rule. First, the realization is that the world is imperfect and people are struggling with debt. All are debtors in one way or another; here the idea is that only God is a creditor as Matthew seems to posit. Except for the master, all are in debt either with the master or among themselves. This worldly situation is compared to the human condition of weakness.

Second, the hope lies in the atypical master in the parable, who understands a difficult situation and forgives debt. In society, this kind of action by the master is not expected. Typically neglecting debt results in punishment or slavery. Matthew's and Jesus' desired action is mercy toward others because society without mercy is hell.

Third, in society there are many unmerciful people like the first slave in this parable who was forgiven with 10,000 denarii. He had a hardened heart and forgot about the forgiveness he received from his master. He did not look into the eyes of his fellow slave friend, who owed him only one hundred denarii, one hundredth of his own debt. For this poor fellow slave even one hundred denarii was too big to pay for unknown reasons (perhaps sickness or family crisis). There is no guarantee that he could pay in full some later time. That is why he does not promise to pay everything, but begs for mercy. This fellow slave really needs mercy without which he and the family cannot live. Actually, earlier the fortunate slave said to his master: "I will pay you everything"! (18:26). He knelt down before the master and asked for an extension of the due date. Apparently he has the ability to pay the debt back if he was given more time. In a way, his situation is not as dire as his fellow's. In fact, the master could have given him an extension. Otherwise, he did not need a complete cancellation of his debt, which he perhaps did not expect. The point is that he was in a better position than his fellow slave. So if anyone needed unconditional mercy, it was his fellow slave, because he cannot pay his debt, even one hundred denarii, now or later. His fellow slave needs this mercy, not him. But this already-forgiven man does not extend mercy to his friend.

Challenge to the Reader

Jesus challenges the reader to have mercy toward others because all are entangled with debt in one way or another. If God is the true good master, all the rest are indebted to God. No one can live in isolation without help from others. People have to show mercy toward others because they all live in an imperfect world where anyone can experience something bad. A fortunate person can reach success one day, but lose it all the next day. This person needs mercy without which there will be no life any more. This is a moment of life or death for that person in need.

An Ideal State of God's Rule

An ideal world perceived by Jesus needs a balanced mind between thanksgiving and humility. Usually, when things go well, people tend to be oblivious to their weakness before God and the world, being drowned in a well of self-deception or narcissism. Even when things go well and smooth, people should have a sense of both joy and humility, because they cannot control their lives by their power. Rather, what they need is a mind of openness and mercy toward others. So when things become rough, they can be helped by others. A new mindset needed for this ideal world goes like this: "The more fortunate I am, the more humble I am."

Father and Two Sons (Luke 15:11–32)[11]

> Then Jesus said, "There was a man who had two sons. The younger of them said to his father, 'Father, give me the share of the property that will belong to me.' So he divided his property between them. A few days later the younger son gathered all he had and traveled to a distant country, and there he squandered his property in dissolute living. When he had spent everything, a severe famine took place throughout that country, and he began to be in need. So he went and hired himself out to one of the citizens of that country, who sent him to his fields to feed the pigs. He would gladly have filled himself with the pods that the pigs were eating; and no one gave him anything. But when he came to himself he said, 'How

---

11. This section is based on my earlier presentation of the paper titled "The Father and Two Sons in Luke 15:11–32" at the 2014 Annual Meeting of Society of Biblical Literature.

many of my father's hired hands have bread enough and to spare, but here I am dying of hunger! I will get up and go to my father, and I will say to him, "Father, I have sinned against heaven and before you; I am no longer worthy to be called your son; treat me like one of your hired hands."' So he set off and went to his father. But while he was still far off, his father saw him and was filled with compassion; he ran and put his arms around him and kissed him. Then the son said to him, 'Father, I have sinned against heaven and before you; I am no longer worthy to be called your son.' But the father said to his slaves, 'Quickly, bring out a robe—the best one—and put it on him; put a ring on his finger and sandals on his feet. And get the fatted calf and kill it, and let us eat and celebrate; for this son of mine was dead and is alive again; he was lost and is found!' And they began to celebrate. "Now his elder son was in the field; and when he came and approached the house, he heard music and dancing. He called one of the slaves and asked what was going on. He replied, 'Your brother has come, and your father has killed the fatted calf, because he has got him back safe and sound.' Then he became angry and refused to go in. His father came out and began to plead with him. But he answered his father, 'Listen! For all these years I have been working like a slave for you, and I have never disobeyed your command; yet you have never given me even a young goat so that I might celebrate with my friends. But when this son of yours came back, who has devoured your property with prostitutes, you killed the fatted calf for him!' Then the father said to him, 'Son, you are always with me, and all that is mine is yours. But we had to celebrate and rejoice, because this brother of yours was dead and has come to life; he was lost and has been found.'" (Luke 15:11–32)

Through the Eyes of Weakness

This famous parable of Jesus has typically been read as an allegory for salvation in that the father represents God, the older son/brother represents Jews or the Pharisees, and the younger son/brother represents newly converted Gentiles. So the traditional emphasis is the father's (God's) abundant love or compassion and the prodigal son's repentance and return. In this light, the older son/brother is seen as a narrow-minded person who does not welcome his brother. But this allegorical reading does not stand when we read this parable as a dysfunctional family story in that the goal of a family is reconciliation, for which mercy of the father is essential.[12] In this light, the main character of the parable is not the lost son but the father whose heart was broken because of his son's senseless departure to a remote region. The father was ready for accepting and welcoming his son no matter what. He did not expect any well-prepared words of repentance from his son. He only wishes for his son's safe return. That is why he waited outside of his home and when he saw his son he ran and kissed him. This father's behavior is unacceptable and atypical in society. Unlike the typical paterfamilias who run the household with authority and power, this father is so weak that he does not prevent his son from leaving home.[13] Furthermore, he waited for his son and welcomed him back without conditions. In a way, he should have reprimanded his son upon his return. But he followed another tradition by having mercy toward his son, because for him the most important thing is to recover the broken family. Toward that goal, what is required by him is not the condition of acceptance but the unconditional welcoming. Justice and reconciliation will happen or must happen after that as time goes by. This act of the father's mercy is possible because his heart was broken already by his son. In other words, his heart runs before his head. This is what we saw in the case of the Samaritan who was first filled with mercy toward the victim.

However, this father is not perfect. If he were perfect, his younger son probably would not need to leave him. As a parent, he was responsible for his son's behavior. Upon his son's return, he did not check with him to know what happened to him. Rather, he was hasty in making a welcome party. He could have slowed down his joy and checked his emotion, preparing such a welcome feast later or the next day after talking with his older and younger sons together. As we know from the story, his older son is completely left out in the process. Nonetheless, this father figure is close to God in terms of his mercy or patience toward his "lost" son. He knows the importance of the whole family together and for that matter, he risks his reputation when

---

12. It is worth hearing Levine's comment on this view of a family story: "In its original context, the parable of the Prodigal Son would not have been heard as a story of repentance or forgiveness, a story of works-righteousness and grace, or a story of Jewish xenophobia and Christian universalism. Instead, the parable's messages of finding the lost, of reclaiming children, of reassessing *the meaning of family* offer not only good news, but better news" (italics are mine). See Levine, *Short Stories by Jesus*, 28.

13. Brandon Scott observes the father image here is like a mother: "The father combines in himself the maternal and paternal roles. As a father he is a failure, but as a mother, he is a success." See Scott, *Hear Then the Parable*, 122.

he unconditionally accepts and welcomes his degenerate son. Only then, restoration or reconciliation of the family can happen. In that regard, this father is a model to follow in a harsh patriarchal society where a strict law of hierarchical unity is exacted without mercy.

The older son/brother is a good son and brother. He is not a hypocrite. He is a hard-working, faithful son. He knows that honor and responsibility are important in the family. From this good son's perspective, his younger brother's behavior is unacceptable. His brother did wrong things. In his mind, if his brother returned home, he should have been punished first. So in some ways, this older son/brother raises the issue of justice and responsibility. He is a good prosecutor concerned with justice in the family. He was angry when he heard that his father gave a big welcome with a big party for his brother. He got home, but did not enter. This also shows that he must be a very thoughtful, patient person. If I were him, I would have run to my brother and grabbed him by both cheeks and said: Why are you here? What did you do? But in fact, he stood outside their home until his father came out to see him.

The father explains to him why he welcomed the younger son and made a feast. The only reason is because he returned home; he was dead and now alive. The big feast was made not because of his good deed or repentance but because of his return. The father found the "dead" one alive now. To the father, both sons are dear and beloved no matter what. There is no familiar ring of typical favoritism of a younger son as in the matriarchs of the Hebrew Bible. The father's point is simple: a family without either son is meaningless and incomplete. Then the father also assures him that his relationship to the older son remains unchanged: "All that is mine is yours" (15:31). I believe that this smart, justice-seeking son understood his father's point about mercy coming before justice or the law. The matter is priority. Since the parable is open-ended, readers actually do not know whether the three-member family eventually reconciled with one another. Ideally, reconciliation of the family or full restoration of the lost son/brother would come gradually.

The Challenge to the Reader

Jesus seems to challenge to people with this parable in saying, "If there is no mercy extended to the socially weak, God's rule will not be possible." Society without mercy is like Rome's rule. There should not be any conditions for acceptance. That is why Jesus, in the gospel stories, eats and talks with the sinners and tax collectors. Jesus did not have any conditions in welcoming the weak. Mercy is first. The father in this parable is a very unconventional patriarch who echoes a loving God full or mercy. He does not prefer an older or younger son. Both of them are equally important to him simply because they are his children. This view of family should extend to that of a bigger community where all members of society ought to be treated equally regardless of their current situations.

An Ideal State of God's Rule

No families or communities are perfect. Therefore, mercy is needed first. Only then may justice be checked and brought back as time goes by. In the end the goal of family is union in peace. Until that goal there should be a process of reconciliation/restoration. Even when one-time resolution or peace is realized, it will not last forever. The process of reconciliation must be cyclical and ongoing. In this dysfunctional family story, the younger son/brother is an icon of a miserable person. He is a bad son who dishonors his father by asking for inheritance before his death.[14] He supposedly does not help his older brother work in the field. He is a selfish, immature man. But he is also a member of the family, so the father accepts him unconditionally and with bountiful mercy. This does not mean that the poor son's sins are forgiven and justice is done because forgiveness and justice must be joined together when this miserable man shows his renewed/restored life as time goes by. This is why the older son's voice of justice is important to the process of reconciliation and needs the changed mind of his younger brother to be effective. Justice should and can be dealt with after mercy comes. When mercy is met by justice, there will be moments of peace—a result of the reconciliation process.

Unjust Judge and Widow (Luke 18:1–8)

Then Jesus told them a parable about their need to pray always and not to lose heart. He said, "In a certain city there was a judge who neither feared God nor had respect for people. In that city there

---

14. In Jewish tradition, inheritance is not transferred until a parent's death (Num 36:7–9; 27:8–11; Sir 33:20–24).

was a widow who kept coming to him and saying, 'Grant (*ekdikeo*) me justice against my opponent.' For a while he refused; but later he said to himself, 'Though I have no fear of God and no respect for anyone, yet because this widow keeps bothering me, I will grant her justice, so that she may not wear me out by continually coming.'" *And the Lord said, "Listen to what the unjust judge says. And will not God grant justice to his chosen ones who cry to him day and night? Will he delay long in helping them? I tell you, he will quickly grant justice to them. And yet, when the Son of Man comes, will he find faith on earth?"* (Luke 18:1–8; italics indicate Luke's redaction and comments)

Through the Eyes of Weakness

The parable proper includes only 18:2–5. The rest (18:1 and 18:6–8) is Luke's interpretation of the parable in which Luke emphasizes the importance of prayer. But in the parable itself the main concern is justice, not prayer.[15] Jesus teaches that the weak have to speak up for justice. The widow says, "Avenge (*ekdikeo*) me justice against my opponent" (18:3). The Greek verb *ekdikeo* conveys a sense of avenge.[16] She addresses an unjust situation in which she is involved and seeks justice. In Jesus' time, widows were among the most vulnerable and the marginalized, along with orphans and foreigners, all who need proper care and protection (Exod 22:22; Deut 10:18; 27:19; Isa 1:17; 10:2; Jer 22:3; Ps 94:6; 146:9; Ezek 22:7; 44:22; Zech 7:9–10; Mal 3:5). This widow is badly situated in a place of daily injustices of which we are not given details. Widows are at the mercy of others and usually passive. But this particular widow in the story is a very atypical character who does not sit and wait for mercy to fall from the sky. She seeks out her justice until it is met. She is challenging society and persistent in her faith that God must hear her.

What is wrong then with the judge in this parable? He is also a very atypical judge, who should have followed a biblical model of a good judge like Moses, fearing God (Ps 111:10; Prov 1:7; Lev 19:14, 32) and respecting people (2 Chr 19:6–7). He should have listened carefully to the voice of the weak, but he was careless and uncaring. His heart was severely hardened. Obviously, this judge is unlike the just God. The irony is that while he does

---

15. Reid, *Parables for Preachers*, 234–35.
16. Levine, *Short Stories by Jesus*, 224.

not fear God, he fears this widow's persistent challenge to him (18:5). Out of his selfish reason, he gives in to her request. It is not out of love or compassion at all. So ironically and eventually, the winner is the widow who is wise and justice-minded, and the loser is the judge who is so silly and self-centered, now knowing what justice is.

The Challenge to the Reader

Through this parable, Jesus seems to teach several things about God's rule. First, the leaders of the community should listen to the voice of the marginalized. They need to think from the weak people's perspective and to listen to them. Jesus seems to say to them: "Break your callous heart and have solidarity with them." Second, Jesus also encourages the marginalized to take up from their place and seek justice by and for themselves, because the world is so evil and leaders are so self-centered that they would not initiate the process of justice for them.

An Ideal State of God's Rule

Since the world is an imperfect place where senseless judges rule without caring for the weak, at least two things are necessary for an ideal world that God rules. First, judges/leaders have to attend to the voices of the weak. Second, if leaders do not do their job, the weak have to rise up to remedy the unjust situation. Here the widow in the parable does not yield to the unjust judge's negligence and bothers him until she is heard. This is a great model of persistent faith for justice.

Rich Farmer (Luke 12:16–21; Thom 63)

> Then he told them a parable: "The land of a rich man produced abundantly. And he thought to himself, 'What should I do, for I have no place to store my crops?' Then he said, 'I will do this: I will pull down my barns and build larger ones, and there I will store all my grain and my goods. And I will say to my soul, 'Soul, you have ample goods laid up for many years; relax, eat, drink, be merry.' But God said to him, 'You fool! This very night your life is being demanded of you. And the things you have prepared, whose will

they be?' So it is with those who store up treasures for themselves but are not rich toward God." (Luke 12:16–21)

Jesus said: There was a rich man who had many possessions. He said: I will use my possessions to sow and reap and plant, to fill my barns with fruit, that I may have need of nothing. Those were his thoughts in his heart; and in that night he died. He who has ears, let him hear. (Thomas 63)

Through the Eyes of Weakness

This parable deals with the issue and conception of community in which both the rich and the poor participate. The problem for this rich farmer is that he is too conscious of himself and his possessions, not being aware of his neighbor's need. This rich man's apparent basis for his happiness is possession. The rich person knows the language of "I" only, and he keeps using "I" (vv. 16–19). With so childish an attitude, he worries about the abundant harvest because his warehouses are not big enough to store everything. So he decides to pull down the current ones and build bigger ones. But Jesus says it is the basis of unhappiness because there is no joy of abundant relationships with his community. Material possession looks good and permanent, but God says: "'You fool! This very night your life is being demanded of you. And the things you have prepared, whose will they be?" (12:20).

The Challenge to the Reader

Jesus challenges the attitude of the rich, who are so self-centered and ignorant of the need of the community. In the end, readers are told that the rich fool's life is miserable because of his abundant harvest that he does not know how to use for other people in the community. The rich farmer makes a critical mistake in that what he has to pull down is not his warehouses but his heart for God and the community, so that he could see and feel the need of others. His heart was callous to the need of others and full of self-centeredness. As a result, the rich man fundamentally fails in his attitude toward God and people. In other words, he does not have a broken spirit (Ps 51). He needed to listen to Jeremiah: "Circumcise yourselves to the Lord, remove the foreskin of your hearts" (Jer 4:4a). He has to break down his selfish mind, not his warehouses to store more. Instead, he should store his overflowing harvest in the warehouses of other people.

An Ideal State of God's Rule

In this parable the ideal world of God's rule ought to begin with a person's realization that he/she is mortal and weak, as God warns the rich farmer: "You fool! This very night your life is being demanded of you. And the things you have prepared, whose will they be?" (12:20). A wise person is someone who always feels and lives with a mindset that he or she will not live forever. If someone seriously thinks that his or her time is so limited, then life can be lived differently. An ideal world re-imagined by Jesus also requires a new mindset about the storage place of wealth. Wealth should not sit idle in the rich man's warehouses. Rather, the abundant harvest must be used for the weak so that their hearts and warehouses are filled with joy. Then the abundant harvest serves all. The rich are happier because of their sharing, and the poor are well fed because of it.

Pharisee and Publican (Luke 18:9–14)

> *He also told this parable to some who trusted in themselves that they were righteous and regarded others with contempt:* "Two men went up to the temple to pray, one a Pharisee and the other a tax collector. The Pharisee, standing by himself, was praying thus, 'God, I thank you that I am not like other people: thieves, rogues, adulterers, or even like this tax collector. I fast twice a week; I give a tenth of all my income.' But the tax collector, standing far off, would not even look up to heaven, but was beating his breast and saying, 'God, be merciful to me, a sinner!' I tell you, this man went down to his home justified rather than the other; *for all who exalt themselves will be humbled, but all who humble themselves will be exalted.*" (Luke 18:9–14; italics indicate Luke's redaction and comments about Jesus' parable)

Through the Eyes of Weakness

The parable proper includes vv. 10–14a. The rest (vv. 9, 14b) may be a Lukan creation that emphasizes the theme of righteousness. This parable deals with the marginalized in society. The setting of the parable is the Temple, which is supposed to be a most holy place, a symbol of God's protection and restoration of Israel. As usual, a Pharisee enters the Temple and prays. His prayer is wordy and overtly thankful for God's grace. Specifically, he thanks God because he keeps the law and does almsgiving regularly. Apparently, his prayer is not wrong. He thanks God for everything about him. But when we see his attitude toward a fellow Jewish man, a tax collector who enters the Temple to pray, his focus turns to a mode of comparison and lacks in mercy or compassion for that "miserable or profane" person. He distances himself from that sinner and takes pride in his difference from him.

In contrast, the tax collector, one of the most marginalized in society—similar to the widow in the parable of the Unjust Judge—enters the Temple with a broken spirit to seek God's mercy. He stands before God, but cannot look up to heaven. His prayer is short and not as beautiful as the Pharisee's prayer. His prayer is an outpouring of the broken spirit, an attitude that is needed toward God. His prayer is a desperate cry for mercy and salvation: "God, be merciful to me, a sinner!" (Luke 18:13). What more can he say than his spirit-broken confession? We need to hear what Laozi similarly observes about the problem in his time: "Truthful words are not beautiful; beautiful words are not truthful."

The Challenge to the Reader

Jesus challenges those who think their righteousness is possible without loving the most profane sinners. Righteousness involves relationships among people; it is not simply a matter of persons to God only. The problem for the Pharisee is that he lacks mercy or a mind of openness to someone who is very different from him. Interestingly, the Pharisee in this parable and the rich farmer in the previous parable have in common the self-focused language of "I." Because of this "I" language and attitude, the Pharisee is blind and cannot see the need of the tax-collector. He cannot see how miserable he may be without God's mercy or grace toward him. So the problem is that he cannot break his spirit or heart toward the poor man. The real problem is that he thinks that he is justified before God without loving undeserving people like the tax-collector.

An Ideal State of God's Rule

The Temple, which is the setting of this parable, is a part of Jesus' ideal world. In Jewish tradition, the temple is the centerpiece of Jewish religious life, especially in terms of prayer. Two men in the parable come to pray. But there are many different kinds or purposes of prayers as we see in the case of Jesus' prayer life: thanksgiving, petition, healing, discernment, and lament. The problem occurs when someone claims only one purpose for praying or limits the function of the temple in order to exclude others. For the Pharisees, the temple is a place of thanksgiving. For the sinner or tax-collector the temple is a place of healing or petition. That is what we see in the tax-collector's prayer requesting mercy of God. The ideal world ruled by God requires a mindset that the temple can cover a full range of humanity from thanksgiving to lament.

Social Activism

To activate God's rule through the eyes of weakness, Jesus not only taught in parables but through public engagement—social activism shown in his breaking boundaries with the profane (i.e., prostitutes, tax collectors, and sinners), restoring human dignity on the Sabbath, cleansing the temple, and welcoming children. In the gospels, Jesus often engages with the most marginalized in society. He talks and eats with them without requiring anything beforehand from them. He breaks the boundary between the sacred and the profane. This creates troubles and tensions between him and the law-bound and purity-concerned people like the Pharisees. The tension is so great that Jesus is accused of intentionally breaking the boundary between the sacred and the profane. News about his social engagements goes out to the villages and other regions, and crowds follow him to hear more about God and to be healed from the illnesses. Sometimes Jesus heals by touching the sick and at other times they touch Jesus' garment. "Touching" is an open act of boundary breaking by Jesus, challenging the division between good and bad. But also the act of boundary breaking is a time of making new relationships with the most marginalized people, who are confirmed as people of God.

Second, controversy on the sabbath has been another hotbed for Jesus since the sabbath laws are too crucial to Jews to be compromised. But once again, to restore humanity back to the original status of creation, Jesus breaks away from the long-held tradition that does not allow for exceptions. As we have seen before, Jesus' point is that the sabbath is for humans, not the other way around. If there is no human dignity on the sabbath, what is the purpose of the sabbath? Jesus seems to reason that if there are wars and injustices in the world then God cannot rest. So healing the sick on the sabbath is to keep the law in its most genuine sense.

Third, the temple cleansing shows Jesus' anger at the malfunction of the temple and his deep focus on the renewal of people. For Jesus the temple is a holy place that provides moral leadership and protection to the people. But in Jesus' time the temple did not function well and was full of sellers of animals for sacrifices and money changers. Leaders of the temple did not care for the poor. Seeing this, Jesus was naturally very upset, and his heart was broken with holy indignation. So he was violent enough to overturn the business tables and expel business people out by whipping them.

Fourth and lastly, Jesus also shows social activism through embracing children, who are a prime example of weakness. Children are weak, physically and spiritually. They are immature and are not considered to be full humans in the time of Jesus. But Jesus takes them up and elevates them as a symbol of genuine humanity. So there is double-sided weakness with children: a plain sense of weakness as an insecurity and a metaphorical sense of weakness as a virtue. Jesus' point is not that they have to be protected only because they are weak, but that they are models for others because they are guileless. Adults are often obstinate with fixed minds. They hardly change their views and instead seek stability.

In Jesus' time who are like children in society? They are none other than those who are heart-broken and marginalized. Their spirit is so severely shattered that they may need God's mercy and God's justice.[17] When people are weak and vulnerable, their eyes are open to God. For them God's rule can settle. So Jesus asks those who are powerful to change their mind. They have to break their spirit and see others before self. Like children needing protection, the weak need the same. But at the same time, the mind of the children and the weak must is a model for the powerful people. That is Jesus' point. For Jesus, an ideal society is achieved through the child-like character of genuine simplicity and a softened, weakened mind that is open to God and others.

---

17. This is why Jesus teaches in Matt 21:31 that the tax collectors and prostitutes enter the kingdom of God ahead of the Pharisees. The reason is that their spirit is broken enough to seek God's mercy and justice. They are ready to follow God's rule.

Healing and Exorcism

Jesus' healing and exorcism also show his solidarity with the weak. In fact, for Jesus there is no separation between his teaching and healing. He teaches about God's rule and at the same time he is involved in healing and exorcisms. Wherever Jesus goes, he meets many sick people, whose bodies and souls are so severely ruined and broken that they can no longer live normally. They are deprived of human dignity and society as a whole does not pay much attention to them. They are like non-humans lying in the shadows of the world that even God's grace may not find them. But Jesus sees inside them the fundamental beauty of God's creation. They are sick now, but they are born as children of God who are supposed to live a most decent life. On the one hand, Jesus must be upset at their realities now, and on the other hand, he must be full of pity and compassion for them and seek full humanity for them.

In this dire situation, what Jesus could do is to offer solace and ask for God's mercy on their behalf. In doing so he was involved in curing them by relieving their anxieties and leading some to the process of healing. The nature of Jesus' healing is, as some scholars believe, close to a "village psychiatrist" who helps the patients deal with their psychosomatic symptoms.[18] In today's medical term, "conversion disorder" may have been dealt with by Jesus. A good number of people have uncontrollable stress or emotional trauma due to personal and social ills that may have caused their illness.

To the sick who were left out from the social "healing" network, Jesus is none other than a savior and healer who cannot pass by them without doing anything.[19] That is to say, Jesus had the enormous capability of empathizing with them. His patients, so to speak, had to believe that they were healed. At least, they are to believe they are fine and will be fine. Perhaps they feel the symptoms of illness are gone forever now. In fact, because of this kind of psychosomatic treatment, Jesus' patients are believed to go through further complete healing over time.

I am not saying, however, that all the healing episodes recorded in the Gospels can be explained this way, nor do I believe that they are all historical. The point is that if the historical Jesus was a healer, his healing activities may look like the picture I described earlier. In other words, I do

---

18. For example, see Capps, *Jesus the Village Psychiatrist*; Dunn, *Jesus and the Spirit*; Howard, *Disease and Healing in the New Testament*; Eve, *The Jewish Context of Jesus' Miracles*; Casey, *Solution to the "Son of Man" Problem*, 144–67.

19. Remus, *Jesus as Healer*.

not believe that Jesus could cure all the sick with all kinds of illnesses. Jesus tradition may have elaborated and embellished the work of Jesus' healing activities, as seen in the Gospels. Without this kind of critical distinction between the actual historical Jesus who was involved in healing in one way or another and the Jesus portrayed in the later Gospels, people are easily led to believe in contrasting ideas: one is that Jesus is seen as a supernatural, charismatic healer who literally cured all as written in the Gospels; or that Jesus is mentally ill with some form of psychopathological disorder. In the former, while some simply believe that Jesus could heal all the sick because he was a divine son of God, others explain that because Jesus was possessed by the Spirit at his baptism he became a charismatic healer.[20] In the case of the latter belief, the three psychiatrists, W. Hirsch, C. Binet-Sangle, and G. L. de Loosten, argue that Jesus was mentally ill and had *paranoia*.[21]

But as I have suggested before, the above two beliefs about Jesus do not even come close to the picture of the historical Jesus' actual ministry based on his experience of weakness and interpretation. Jesus was obviously a human; though, he was extraordinary in many respects. Although Jesus' baptism was an important event to him, I do not believe that Jesus was possessed by the Spirit once and for all, capable of all his powerful work just because of that one-time special power descending, as Stevan Davies believes. Marcus Borg's view of the Spirit-filled Jesus may be close to the historical Jesus in the sense that Jesus continued to maintain his special relationship with the Spirit.

Regarding the view that Jesus was mentally ill, as Albert Schweitzer already rebutted the three psychiatrists' claim, there is no evidence in the texts that Jesus was mentally ill.[22] The gospel texts have to be critically examined whether they are coming from Jesus or from later times. Also, they should not project their modern view of mental illness to Jesus without looking at the first-century cultural context of healers.[23]

Schweitzer's critique is exegetically sound, but even his careful view of Jesus needs discussion since he says that Jesus had a high estimate of himself

---

20. Davies, *Jesus the Healer*, 104.

21. Binet-Sangle, *La Folie de Jesus*; Hirsch, *Religion und Civilisation*; Loosten, *Jesus Christus*.

22. Schweitzer, *Psychiatric Study of Jesus*, 81.

23. See Eve, *Jewish Context of Jesus' Miracles*. He argues that Shaman in Korea may be a similar example that Jesus played in his time.

and that "perhaps the hallucination happened at the baptism."[24] Jesus must have had high estimate of himself because all of creation is God's. But I do not think, as I argued in chapters 2–3, that his high view of himself is sealed or separate from his lowly, marginalized experience. Rather, he must have had some form of cognitive dissonance between his ideal self and real self because his life was miserable and his self-esteem was ruined and challenged. In other words, Jesus' high view of himself must be understood from the other side of his marginal experience due to his family and social background. More than that, Jesus finds a new source of energy because of his lowly life experience. Regarding his view of the hallucination at Jesus' baptism, it is hard to tell what exactly happened to Jesus. But again, I do not think his baptism experience is naïve or due to hallucination. Although we cannot describe the psyche of Jesus at the baptism, one thing we can safely say is that his experience becomes a watershed event to which he devotes his life for the renewal of people and Israel.

Then what is my view? My view is that Jesus was a healer, yes, but that Jesus can be explained or understood from both his extraordinary capability of empathizing with others and his conviction about God's power of healing. In the following we will see a few healing episodes to identify how Jesus is involved in his healing. In doing so, there are a few caveats. First, we should know that Jesus' healing activity happens while he is engaged in his proclamation ministry of God's rule. In other words, healing itself is not the goal of his ministry. Second, there is also a general pattern about his healing process: encountering, moved with compassion, action (speak or touch), and blessing (go in peace). Third, not all healing episodes recorded in the Gospels are historical and most of them are believed to be embellished to communicate the importance of faith in order for the person to be healed and to demonstrate the healing power of Jesus. With these caveats in mind, we consider some representative healing episodes in Mark, which are also found in Matthew and Luke.

Healing Simon's Mother-in-Law
(Mark 1:29–31; Matt 8:14–15; Luke 4:38–39)

> As soon as they left the synagogue, they entered the house of Simon and Andrew, with James and John. Now Simon's mother-in-law

---

24. Schweitzer, *Psychiatric Study of Jesus*, 81.

was in bed with a fever, and they told him about her at once. He came and took her by the hand and lifted her up. Then the fever left her, and she began to serve them. (Mark 1:29–31)

When Jesus entered Peter's house, he saw his mother-in-law lying in bed with a fever; he touched her hand, and the fever left her, and she got up and began to serve him. (Matt 8:14–15)

After leaving the synagogue he entered Simon's house. Now Simon's mother-in-law was suffering from a high fever, and they asked him about her. Then he stood over her and rebuked the fever, and it left her. Immediately she got up and began to serve them. (Luke 4:38–39)

The setting of Jesus' healing is his Galilean ministry of teaching about God's rule. He taught in the synagogue at Capernaum and then entered the house of Simon and Andrew, with James and John. We do not know why he entered there, but one possible conjecture is that Jesus knew Simon's mother-in-law already because Simon is his disciple. Perhaps Jesus entered there to rest a bit. Immediately Jesus is told about her illness. We do not know how long she was in bed because of a fever. Then Jesus "came and took her by the hand and lifted her up" (Mark 1:31). Matthew changes Mark and omits "lifted her up," having only "touched her." Matthew's motivation for changing this is supposedly to emphasize Jesus' power of healing. Luke goes one step further and states that Jesus only commands and does not touch her at all ("rebuked the fever" Luke 4:39). The Markan version of the healing looks the closest to the historical Jesus. Mark 1:31 records three steps in Jesus' healing: coming, taking her by the hand, and lifting her up. "Coming" indicates Jesus' agreement to the disciples' request for her healing. Though the text does not have the word "pity" connected to Jesus, he comes with pity. Simon's mother-in-law, on the other hand, is stuck in bed with a fever although she really wanted to help Jesus' ministry. Upon coming to her, Jesus takes her by the hand and lifts her up. This is one simultaneous action. Jesus held her hand and helped her rise up. This is Jesus' healing action by faith. He did not simply pray for healing or did not wait for healing. He acted by touching her and lifting her up from the bed. At that moment of Jesus' spiritual connection with her, perhaps the power of healing worked for her. What we learn from this healing story is that Jesus took side with her weakness, and then he showed his faith for healing through physical and spiritual contact with her. At the same time, healing does not happen only in one way. She was eager to help Jesus' ministry. Healing is not a one-way business but a mutual business of relationship between a healer and the one who is healed.

Cleansing a Leper (Mark 1:40–45; Matt 8:1–4; Luke 5:12–16)

> A leper came to him begging him, and kneeling he said to him, "If you choose, you can make me clean." *Moved with pity*, Jesus stretched out his hand and touched him, and said to him, "I do choose. Be made clean!" Immediately the leprosy left him, and he was made clean. After sternly warning him he sent him away at once, saying to him, "See that you say nothing to anyone; but go, show yourself to the priest, and offer for your cleansing what Moses commanded, as a testimony to them." But he went out and began to proclaim it freely, and to spread the word, so that Jesus could no longer go into a town openly, but stayed out in the country; and people came to him from every quarter. (Mark 1:40–45)

> When Jesus had come down from the mountain, great crowds followed him; and there was a leper who came to him and knelt before him, saying, "Lord, if you choose, you can make me clean." He stretched out his hand and touched him, saying, "I do choose. Be made clean!" Immediately his leprosy was cleansed. Then Jesus said to him, "See that you say nothing to anyone; but go, show yourself to the priest, and offer the gift that Moses commanded, as a testimony to them." (Matt 8:1–4)

> Once, when he was in one of the cities, there was a man covered with leprosy. When he saw Jesus, he bowed with his face to the ground and begged him, "Lord, if you choose, you can make me clean." Then Jesus stretched out his hand, touched him, and said, "I do choose. Be made clean." Immediately the leprosy left him. And he ordered him to tell no one. "Go," he said, "and show yourself to the priest, and, as Moses commanded, make an offering for your cleansing, for a testimony to them." But now more than ever the word about Jesus spread abroad; many crowds would gather to hear him and to be cured of their diseases. But he would withdraw to deserted places and pray. (Luke 5:12–14)

Jesus' continued journey of teaching God's rule throughout Galilee is the setting of this healing. This time a leper suddenly appears on the scene of

Jesus' mission journey and seeks healing from him. While Matthew and Luke state that the leper addresses Jesus as Lord, Mark does not. The reason may be that both Matthew and Luke are concerned with Christology and thus "Lord" is important. But in the original healing episode, calling Jesus Lord may not have happened.

There is also a small difference in terms of how the leper approached Jesus. While Matthew says that the leper "came and knelt," Luke says that he "bowed with his face to the ground and begged." It may be the case that Matthew refines Mark's three modes of movement ("coming, begging, and kneeling") to make the text simple. Luke changes Mark more than Matthew, making the leper show the highest honor to Jesus by bowing with his face to the ground. All this implies that both Matthew and Luke are concerned with Christology in the sense that the leper knows that Jesus is Lord. But in Mark there is no immediate clue about such christological consideration in Matthew and Luke.[25] The leper shows his earnest and desperate need of healing, which is indicated with his three modes of movement: "coming," "begging," and "kneeling": "A leper came to him begging him, and kneeling he said to him" (Mark 1:40a). Even before he uttered what he wanted exactly, he showed urgency with his bodily gesture. In the story setting, these three divisions do not seem redundant because they show the leper's situation, where he comes to beg for his healing and if it does not go well, he kneels, and makes a final petition. In other words, in Mark we can see his most natural gesture and mind that shows his desperate need. This act shows that he is ready to be healed, and he just needs someone's blessing or confirmation on behalf of God. Having leprosy, he was like a dead person in the community. His spirit probably broke down many times. That is where he is now, standing before Jesus about whom he heard.

Finally, he says: "If you choose, you can make me clean." In Mark, as we have seen before, there is no "Lord" before "if you choose." Otherwise, the three Gospels have the same words. The leper's request is somewhat ironic given the fact that he showed the urgency of his healing. He could have made a more blunt request: Make me clean! But his language is rather gentle and does not show his desperate need for healing because he gives Jesus the freedom to choose. But from another angle, this soft language was possible because he had confidence in Jesus and God's healing power.

---

25. In Mark, the view of Christology is very human Jesus. He denies to be called good. The only one who is good is God (Mark 10:18).

Now Jesus was "moved with pity" (this part appears only in Mark) and "stretched out his hand and touched him, and said to him, 'I do choose. Be made clean!" (Mark 1:41; Matt 8:3; Luke 5:13). Jesus' gesture (stretching out his hand and touching him) is a nice match and response to the leper's coming, begging, and kneeling. Jesus met him with his hand and finally confirmed what the leper wanted: "I do choose. Be made clean" (Mark 1:41; Matt 8:3; Luke 5:13). But in Mark Jesus is "moved with pity" (*splanchnistheis*), which is the aorist participle of *splanchnizomai* ("to have pity or compassion").[26] This part is important for knowing who Jesus is or what he felt at this time; "pity" is what characterizes him. Jesus "had pity" (the aorist verb *esplanchnisthe*) for weak people and because of his pity he continued to heal and teach about God's rule (Mark 6:34; Matt 9:36; 14:14; Luke 7:13). Jesus felt bad when he saw so many people not being taken care of, so the text says: "As he went ashore, he saw a great crowd; and he had *compassion for them*, because they were like sheep without a shepherd; and he began to teach them many things" (Mark 6:34). Jesus acted toward the "lost or weak" by means of his own sense of weakness that is identified with them.

Through this same pity, Jesus saw the leper and identified with his broken spirit. When the leper came, begged, and knelt before Jesus, Jesus was also ready to heal him because he was filled with pity. Pity is a starting point for Jesus to be involved in healing. Similarly, the Samaritan in one of Jesus' parables had pity before he helped the victim (Luke 10:33), and the father in a different parable of Jesus had pity on his younger son (Luke 15:32). It is the same pity with which all of them started to work. The leper and Jesus were one at that moment because they were weak and confident about God's healing and restoration.

Healing a Woman's Hemorrhage
(Mark 5:25–34; Matt 9:19–22; Luke 8:43–48)

Now there was a woman who had been suffering from hemorrhages for twelve years. She had endured much under many physicians, and had spent all that she had; and she was no better, but rather grew worse. She had heard about Jesus, and came up behind him in the crowd and touched his cloak, for she said, "If I but touch his clothes, I will be made well." Immediately her

---

26. *Splanchnizomai* ("to have compassion or pity") also appears in Mark 8:2 and Matt 15:32. The aorist participle is also found in Matt 18:27 and 20:34.

hemorrhage stopped; and she felt in her body that she was healed of her disease. Immediately aware that power had gone forth from him, Jesus turned about in the crowd and said, "Who touched my clothes?" And his disciples said to him, "You see the crowd pressing in on you; how can you say, 'Who touched me?'" He looked all around to see who had done it. But the woman, knowing what had happened to her, came in fear and trembling, fell down before him, and told him the whole truth. He said to her, "Daughter, your faith has made you well; go in peace, and be healed of your disease." (Mark 5:25–34)

This healing episode appears in all three Synoptic Gospels and their differences are inconsequential so we will not compare them. The setting of this healing is somewhat similar to that of the above two healing episodes in terms of Jesus' ongoing mission journey about God's rule. He was busy teaching about God and was moving to other places to do more work of God. Then Jairus, one of the leaders of the synagogue, appears and asks Jesus to heal his daughter. So Jesus goes with him, and a large crowd follows Jesus and presses in on him. At this moment, suddenly, a woman who had suffered from hemorrhages for twelve years appears on the scene. The text says that she did everything she could to cure her disease with help of the physicians, but her situation grew worse. She heard about Jesus and came to him, but soon realized that it was difficult to stop Jesus because there were too many people following him. She said to herself: "If I but touch his clothes, I will be made well" (Mark 5:28). Like the leper who was healed before, this woman was desperate to be healed since she suffered for so long. She needed the slightest touch of divine grace, which she believes is offered through Jesus. Immediately she felt she was healed. That is it. She was healed through her faith without Jesus' act or agreement. The healing episode could have ended here.

But that is not the case. Immediately, Jesus knows that power had gone from him and asked who touched him. Jesus says someone touched him, but actually the woman touched his garment. Jesus sensed a touch, however meager it would be, because he felt power going out. It is interesting that Jesus is not in control of his power! How is it possible or how can we explain her healing without Jesus' action? It is possible, as I said before, because the woman was ready to be healed through her faith in God; and she needed only a slight moment of divine grace. She needed only even a meager touch of Jesus, the son of God. Healing is not controlled by Jesus, but comes from God through the presence and work of Jesus. At the final scene, the woman who touched Jesus said the whole truth. Then Jesus affirms her faith and blesses her: "Daughter, your faith has made you well; go in peace, and be healed of your disease" (Mark 5:34).

Summary

Jesus activates God's rule through a renewed understanding and practice of weakness that surrounds him and the world. In this chapter we have seen examples of his engagement in the world through his parables, social activism, and healing. The select parables were analyzed with a focus on the lens of weakness. Namely, we have seen how weakness can be explored in them, what challenges Jesus aims to give to the reader, and what Jesus perceives as an ideal world of God's rule. For example, using the seed parable, Jesus reminds the readers the importance of smallness in God's rule. Using the leaven parable, Jesus reminds his audience of the importance of hiddenness in God's rule, so that the weak can play an important role as they are embraced in the work of God. Using the father and two sons parable, Jesus reminds his audience of the importance of mercy in God's rule, in which the weak can be embraced without conditions. In all of Jesus' parables one important virtue in God's rule is mercy. Jesus' social activism is also an expression of Jesus' love of God's rule in which the weak ought to be restored to normalcy. When the Temple does not function as it should, Jesus turns over the money-changers' tables. On the Sabbath, people have to rest with God and sing hallelujahs in unison. If that does not happen on such a holy day, Jesus heals the sickening body and soul. Jesus' healing episodes also demonstrate his love of the weak. On the one hand, Jesus shows solidarity with the weak in society and empowers them to live as child of God. On the other hand, he challenges those with hardened hearts to be weak before God and others.

6

Jesus' Crucifixion as a Paradox of Weakness

THE PURPOSE OF THIS chapter is to explore Jesus' death in view of weakness variously understood in this book. That is, Jesus lived in a scary world where Rome was in control of Palestine with military might. People in miserable situations due to political suppression and economic exploitation experience all kinds of weakness in the world. In this harsh world, Jesus sees the world through the eyes of weakness and begins his ministry for the weak. The end is, however, his death—not just any death but a horrific death by crucifixion. Jesus may have hoped that people would accept his message and change their minds, but things did not go in the direction he wished. Later he realized that he came too far in his journey and felt that he could be imprisoned or even killed because of his bold teaching and action about God's rule over against against Rome's rule. As Mark clearly portrays, Jesus feels agitated due to his impending perils. He did not want torture or any form of suffering, not to mention death. It is simply bad, and it does not carry any value; however, Jesus did not stop doing his work as usual. Perhaps he believed that God would be with him to the end. Perhaps he did not expect that he would be captured and executed. Even on this seemingly unstable journey, Jesus may have thought of his plausible death as a holy, heroic death.

As more time goes by, Jesus was captured and tried before Pilate. He received a death penalty of crucifixion. From that time on, Jesus may have thought about his death differently because his crucifixion was more tangible. What did he feel then? How can we understand his experience of the cross in view of weakness? These are the main questions that we have to deal with in this chapter. One aspect to keep in mind is that no one dimension or level of Jesus' crucifixion, or no one perspective or interpretation, can sufficiently address everything about his death. Jesus himself must have been going through varied emotions and interpretations about his crucifixion. For example, at one point he is hesitant to continue on his journey as we see from his prayer at Gethsemane. But he decides to go on with his work of God, being adamant about his call from God, and therefore being ready to die in order to preach God's good news. At still other times he must have felt that he was completely abandoned because there was no savior or help from heaven when he was hung on the cross.

Jesus' Crucifixion as a Paradox of Weakness

Overall, Jesus' crucifixion presents a paradox of weakness. On the one hand, it is clearly a tragedy, a result of weakness and carried out by Rome. As Paul says, Jesus was crucified out of weakness (2 Cor 13:4). But this also means that he was executed by Rome. In this sense, he is a victim of political powers. With this view, Jesus' crucifixion is a bad thing and should not have happened. Obviously, he did not aim to die on the cross. The best thing for Jesus was to preach the good news of God without being harmed or killed. But his word and action about God's rule were considered a potential threat and so he was removed. Because of the sudden end of his life, Jesus did not complete what he wanted to accomplish: the full coming of God's rule in the here and now.

On the other hand, he lived with weakness, advocating for the weak, teaching about God's rule, not Rome's rule. Jesus was willing to die for God and his rule, knowing the stakes were high. In this sense, he died a holy death of love. At the same time, Jesus' crucifixion raises questions about theodicy. With all of this in mind, we will have to explore more specific implications about weakness's relations to Jesus' death.

Jesus' Crucifixion out of Weakness

This idea that Jesus "was crucified by weakness" comes from Paul and his bluntly clear view of Jesus' crucifixion (2 Cor 13:4a). Paul is right in his view of Jesus' death in relation to weakness. One of the main issues with interpretation of 2 Cor 13:4a is how to translate and understand *ex astheneias*. While I translate is as "by weakness," others, such as the NRSV, translate it as "in weakness" to implicate Jesus' voluntary suffering. But the primary meaning of the preposition *ex* means "from, by, by means of, or by reason of." If Paul wanted to say that Jesus suffered and was crucified *in weakness*, he would have used the preposition *en* instead of *ex*: *en astheneia*. But what we see from Paul is *ex astheneias*, which can be translated/understood as "from weakness" (weakness being the source of his crucifixion) or as "by weakness" (weakness being the cause of his crucifixion). While it is not easy to distinguish between the source and cause of Jesus' crucifixion in conjunction with weakness, weakness as the source of his crucifixion may have to do with human weakness in general. Though Jesus is the Messiah ("the anointed one") and the Son of God, he is still a human being who is vulnerable to violence. So Paul seems to recognize the fact that Jesus was not superhuman or divine in that he could not prevent his crucifixion by strength. On the other hand, weakness as the cause of Jesus' crucifixion has more to do with his bold and radical challenge to Rome and Jerusalem. In other words, Roman power was too strong to be defeated by Jesus' teaching or deeds. He could not defeat violent authorities because he was weak. Actually, Jesus' plan is not to topple the regime by military might or violence. His teaching and deeds about God could not win over the people and powers because they did not like them. The fact that he could not defeat the evil powers and he was crucified is because he was weak. This view holds that Jesus' weakness led to his crucifixion. If Jesus had been perfect or almighty like God, he would not have been crucified because God cannot be killed or defeated by evil powers. Or, Jesus could have persuaded or led authorities and people to change their mind and accept his message of good news. But that did not happen.

With this consequential view of Jesus' crucifixion, Paul seems to emphasize a few things. First, Jesus did his best as the Son of God and the Messiah and he was crucified because of weakness. Second, Jesus was crucified not simply because he was weak, but because there was imperial, inhumane, evil powers that struck him down. This is why Jesus' crucifixion involves God's judgment in that God judges those responsible for Jesus' crucifixion. Any Christology or theory of atonement that does not consider this fact seriously is a great distortion to the study of the historical Jesus.[1] Even with feminist theology, which raises critical interpretive questions about Jesus' crucifixion, feminist theologians do not see a part of God's judgment in the

---

1. To this group of distortion belong atonement theories developed after Jesus' death and for a long period of time such as ransom theory, penal substitution theory, or satisfaction theory.

event of the cross, not to mention the painful failure of Jesus' "kingdom" preaching out of weakness.[2] Rather, in one way or another they emphasize some positive aspects of Christian theology in relation to Jesus' death. For example, there are several attempts to understand the meaning of Jesus' crucifixion with a focus on God's redemptive suffering through Jesus' death,[3] on God's solidarity with the marginalized,[4] on Jesus' self-giving love,[5] or on the divine *eros* or the divine beauty in faces of people.[6]

Third, beyond Jesus' crucifixion by weakness or God's judgment, Paul declares that Jesus (crucified) "lives *by the power of God*" (2 Cor 13:4b), which is paralleled and contrasted with "crucified *by weakness*" (2 Cor 13:4a). On the one hand, as we saw before, Paul states that Jesus did his best proclaiming God's good news concerning God's rule, not Rome's rule. Out of weakness and by evil hands Jesus was crucified and stopped. Apparently, he failed in his mission. It is true that he could not complete his mission if that was to change the world. Jesus is no more on earth and he not only failed his mission but was abandoned by God. But on the other hand, Paul says that it is God who makes the crucified Jesus alive. This means that God acknowledges Jesus' work and vindicates him. Even though Jesus was defeated by weakness and evil powers and people, God says that Jesus did not fail because his legacy of faithful obedience to God could continue with generations to come.

Jesus' Crucifixion as Holy Death of Love

Jesus' crucifixion has another dimension that we have to consider. That is, Jesus' crucifixion is considered the holy death of love. But the issue is how

---

2. Paul does not seem to think that Jesus completed his mission because "completion" means that a good number of people, if not all, accept Jesus' message and change their mind toward God's rule. In this sense, Jesus' crucifixion leaves people to be bewildered about his messianic work. From a Jewish perspective, as Paul himself thought before his conversion or call, Jesus' crucifixion is evidence that he failed. His mission did not bring in a big change in people's lives or in national political life. Even from Jesus' own perspective, he may have thought that his crucifixion was a premature one because things did not change fast enough as he expected. Rather, what he faced was obstacles after another one.

3. This idea is a continuation of traditional atonement theories as we saw before.

4. This view is, for example, taken by liberation theologians according to whom Jesus shows his solidarity with the oppressed.

5. Among others, see Mercedes, *Power For*.

6. Farley, *Gathering Those Driven Away*.

we understand this "holy death of love."[7] Different theological traditions have varying views about this. For example, traditional atonement theories such as ransom, penal substitution, or satisfaction theories view Jesus' crucifixion as a necessary sacrifice for individual salvation.[8] Whether the reason for Jesus' death is the devil's control of sinners (ransom theory), the need to pay the price of sin (penal substitution), or the need to satisfy God's moral justice (satisfaction theory), all of these atonement theories require Jesus' death (not necessarily crucifixion). Here the holy death of love can be understood in twofold way: God's love that allows his Son to be sent to the world and to die for salvation of individuals and Jesus' love of God and the world by giving his life (meaning his death). But there are many problems with these atonement theories, which were developed over a long period of time (for example, the satisfaction theory came out of the ninth and tenth centuries) and are still cherished by many Christians.

(1) There is no critical consideration or discussion about weakness that involves Jesus as a Jewish prophet or holy man. There is no human struggle in these views; rather, their whole emphasis is the "literal" incarnation that God became Jesus and took the form of weakness.[9] So Jesus' death is considered the most holy-love-death in that Jesus endured suffering in weakness.

(2) All of these traditional views require Jesus' death (just a death), because for various reasons described before, it is necessary for individual salvation. In these views it is said that Jesus came to die for

---

7. For example, Dale Allison links the holy death of love with Jesus' committed and determined life for bringing in the kingdom of God through his work. For that apocalyptic mission, Jesus was willing to die. See Allison, *Constructing Jesus*, 433. On the other hand, Richard Horsley thinks of Jesus' death as a tragically prophetic one because Jesus was involved in world-shattering challenge to the status quo. So Jesus' holy death of love is seen in his tragic death, which is the result of what he has done. See Horsley, *Jesus and Empire*, 35–54. A host of other scholars may think of Jesus' holy death of love as his voluntary salvific death. Therefore the question is how to understand the aspect of "holy death of love" for Jesus.

8. For information about the traditional atonement theories in general, see Aulen, *Christus Victor*. See also Baillie, *God Was in Christ*.

9. See Kim, *Truth, Testimony, and Transformation*. I distinguish between "literal" incarnation and metaphorical incarnation. The former means that God became Jesus, literally. The latter means that God is seen or testified through the life of Jesus. Jesus embodies God's presence in the world. Otherwise, he himself is not the God incarnate. Rather, he incarnates God's love in the world.

sinners. But Jesus came not to die but "to testify to the truth" of God (John 18:37) or "to proclaim the good news of God" (Mark 1:14).

(3) They all focus on individual salvation, disregarding the need of recovery of community or cosmos. But Paul yearned for a cosmic redemption by living the way of God. There is not so much talk of justice in this world. Even if they are concerned with this world, it still is secondary, a place of transitory staying to show the greatness of God.

(4) Likewise, the primary concept of individual salvation is based on a dualism between this world and the next world, or between body and soul. But Jesus never preached that God's kingdom or rule is in heaven. His primary concern and hope is that God's rule be established on earth.

(5) Their view of God is terrifying in the sense that he sent the Son to be killed in order to save people. In this view God not only planned such a horrible thing but watched the senseless, merciless torture of Jesus. Again, in the canonical Gospels there are no direct references or claims about this kind of God who sent his Son to be killed for salvation.

(6) Their view of Jesus is also problematic because Jesus' humanity is deprived in their atonement theories. Again, Jesus' purpose of life is not to die for sinners but to teach about God's rule, not Rome's rule. In his mission journey, Jesus wants his message and work to be accepted by all so that God's rule may come to earth powerfully. Early in his mission, he probably did not expect that he was going to die because of his good works for God and the world. Ignoring the human side of Jesus' anxiety or suffering does a great injustice to Jesus.

Even in modern day theological circles, the overall picture is not very different from the traditional atonement theories. It is especially true for the fundamentalist or the so-called evangelical theological circles. But liberal, liberationist, feminist theologians challenge the old paradigm of the interpretation of the cross and criticize all traditional abusive theologies of the cross that condone evil or injustice. To see this challenging trend, I will briefly examine the works of a few feminist theologians and point out their limitations. First, Anna Mercedes argues that a renewed understanding of Jesus' self-giving on the cross would be helpful to forming a new, liberating, transformative identity. Traditionally, the idea of self-giving on the cross was understood mainly as a loss of the self, identity or agency. But she insists that self-giving can be done voluntarily, out of his or her love for others. She sees *kenosis* ("emptying of the self") as a power that "leans toward others and offers itself to them"[10] and that "may enable the very flourishing of the self."[11] In her view, the cross is an event where God's self-giving and Jesus' self-giving are incarnated in good ways.

While it is important to see the positive side of self-giving, the problem is that Jesus' cross is also a tragic event—the result of state torture done on the innocent. In that sense, we do not see Jesus' self-giving but the ruin of him. Rather, if we have to locate examples of Jesus' self-giving, we have to look more closely at Jesus' ministry that eventually led to his death. Out of mercy and love, Jesus taught about God's rule and healed many. That is a great example of self-giving to God. His death, precisely his crucifixion, may be an unfortunate end to his self-giving life, but the cross itself is not the culmination of his self-giving life. Rather, it is a tragic event. The cause of Jesus' crucifixion has to do with his work for God and the world. His death is not the example of his self-giving. If we do not distinguish between the cause and result of his cross, our view of Jesus would be both limited and twisted because we would fail to see the horrible tragedy of Jesus' death, even going so far as to condone evil and injustices done to Jesus and others.

Second, Arnfridur Gudmundsdottir reads Jesus' cross in view of God's suffering and compassion for human beings, as she observes: "Only a suffering God who out of love chooses to suffer with suffering people brings hope for those who suffer."[12] She emphasizes that God's love is shown through the suffering of Jesus because in it God also suffers not only with Jesus but with humanity as a whole. She understands that because of God's suffering love that identifies with all human suffering, people are hopeful about their lives and encouraged to follow a God whose love wins over violence or evil. In her view, this voluntary suffering love of God is seen in Jesus' cross. Jesus, who is God incarnate, voluntarily suffers for humanity in weakness. Otherwise, Jesus was not weak but was a strong God.

While readers may see the side of God's compassion at the event of the cross, the puzzle is over how God can suffer in good ways at the presence of injustices. Can such a God condone evil or injustices done to Jesus? So the big problem is, again, as we saw in the case of Mercedes, there is no critical

---

10. Mercedes, *Power For*, 7.
11. This quote is from a review of Mercedes's book. Webb, "Power in Weakness."
12. Gudmundsdottir, *Meeting God on the Cross*, 155.

articulation about the cause and result of Jesus' crucifixion. Jesus' suffering on the cross is the result of his mission journey, in his teaching and healing. Otherwise, his suffering does not have intrinsic value. This focus on the suffering of Jesus in connection with the divine suffering and compassion shows a great distortion in the work of the historical Jesus, who does not seem to believe that he simply came to suffer for humanity on the cross. Rather, he came to testify to the truth or to proclaim the good news of God, not the good news of Rome or Jerusalem.

Third, Wendy Farley approaches Jesus' cross, in view of divine incarnation of love and her view of the cross, is very different from Gudmundsdottir's approach, which emphasizes the redemptive, vicarious, and transformative suffering of God and Jesus.[13] Farley sees in Jesus' voluntary cross the divine beauty in all people. This reading is to see the other side of Jesus' cross, which tells us that no sufferings can prevent the divine face in all of us. In other words, it is not suffering that is holy, but it is Jesus' love for humanity that is not defeated by all kinds of torture. Jesus' love takes him down to a rock-bottom experience of hell on the cross. Instead of vicarious suffering, she observes this beautifully: "Suffering tells us we are unredeemable. The passion tells us that we are saved and always were and always will be."[14] This reading of Farley keeps a good balance between the difficulties of suffering and the theological significance of Jesus' suffering and in doing so, she clearly says that suffering itself is not salvific. Rather, suffering is bad, and the true form of salvation begins with the recognition that love wins. All are beautiful creatures of God. But I wish she would explore more Jesus' love on the cross in view of his ministry of God's rule. Unless she does so, the formidable weakness lies in the fact that Jesus' crucifixion is romanticized in terms of his love.

Fourth, M. Shawn Copeland interprets Jesus' cross from the perspective of African Americans going through the demonization and dehumanization that ranges from slavery to racism.[15] She sees in the cross the inhumane, horrible suffering of Jesus and connects it with the suffering of African Americans. Then she jumps to the conclusion that Jesus' suffering is in solidarity with the oppressed. This reading is certainly plausible and is well accepted among liberation theologians. Through his horrible death, Jesus identifies with the marginalized, the tortured, and oppressed. Unlike

13. Farley, *Gathering Those Driven Away*.
14. Ibid., 164.
15. Copeland, *Enfleshing Freedom: Body*.

the feminists discussed previously, Copeland clearly describes Jesus' death as a tragic event where his body was desecrated, and in doing so, she emphasizes Jesus' self-giving love for "the exploited, despised, and poor."[16] But one major problem with her reading is that she discusses neither the evil hands behind Jesus' death nor God's judgment against those responsible for Jesus' death. In this regard, her reading is also susceptible to my earlier critique of other feminist theologians. That is, suffering is evil and bad if it is connected with Jesus' teaching and deed. Jesus' suffering or torture is not the expression of love but the consequence of his work. In this regard, we have to say that Jesus' suffering is not only unwanted but wrong. Overall, feminist theologians modified traditional views of atonement theories in good yet limited ways, seeing God's compassion and Jesus' love on the cross, emphasizing the need of self-giving and inclusive love of the oppressed and the marginalized. But what the majority ignore about Jesus' death is the fact that Jesus was *crucified*. What really matters is not simply that he died, but that he was crucified by Rome and out of weakness.

In the following, I will be clear about what I mean by the holy death of love. I do not mean that Jesus offered himself as a sacrifice for God to bring in God's apocalyptic end to the world. For instance, Albert Schweitzer argues that Jesus threw himself in harm's way as a form of sacrifice to expedite the dawning of God's rule. However, Jesus' primary concern is not about when the kingdom comes, but how it is established in the here and now, as he tells us in Luke 17:21.[17] Jesus is a counter-cultural reformer or social prophet who is more interested in the lives of people in the here and now. Even though apocalypticism is a main current in the days of first-century Judaism, there is no guarantee that Jesus must have taken the same view as the majority.

Jesus' holy death of love is different from the aspects of atonement that we saw before in the voluntary, vicarious suffering for humanity. Jesus was not destined for death; his primary mission was to testify to the truth and to proclaim the good news of God, which is about God's rule, not Rome's rule. So Jesus' crucifixion is not necessary for salvation.[18] Rather, it is a painful

---

16. Ibid., 99.

17. Kim, *Resurrecting Jesus*.

18. In the New Testament as a whole, the concept of salvation varies. However, in the four Gospels the emphasis is not the so-called otherworldly salvation of the soul. In general, salvation there means wholeness: to be whole or to have right relationships with God. In this sense, salvation can be achieved by repenting and seeking God's will. In that salvation there is no place of Jesus' death. Forgiveness is possible when people forgive

tragic event, which paradoxically shows Jesus' faith and love because he did not recant or give up on his journey for God's rule. Nonetheless, it is a tragic event that he did not choose or want. Therefore, we have to make a distinction between voluntary suffering or death and unwanted death. Even though the best scenario for Jesus was to deliver God's good news without being harmed or killed, that wish of Jesus did not work out as the Gospel stories tell us. Jesus' blood, however, is not necessary for human salvation. Jesus' blood is precious not because he was God or because he shed blood for salvation of humanity but because it is a God-given life that cannot be tortured and maimed by anyone or authority. Therefore the holy death of love by Jesus is not based in his suffering death itself but rooted in his unyielding faithfulness to the truth of God for which he risked his life. Jesus should be examined over the course of his entire life, not just his crucifixion. Along the road of his mission, he did not recant his belief and vision about God and the world. The result is a painful torture and death on the cross in which we can see his unwavering love of God.

Jesus' Crucifixion as Weakness that Demands Justice

There is still another dimension to Jesus' crucifixion demanding discussion: the justice of God. The question is why a good God allows evil to be rampant. Jesus did his best despite his humanity and embodied God's love in the world. Yet, the result is so painful that Jesus was executed. There must be God's judgment that holds people and powers behind Jesus' death accountable. Evil is evil and it should be judged and punished. That is a form of justice. Forgiveness can be offered in the name of mercy of God, but it should not be confused with condoning injustices or evil done to the victims. From the human side, forgiveness is a decision that we do not retaliate against the offenders without going through the justice system. God judges those who are responsible for Jesus' death.

Even with God's judgment concerning the cross, there is still an indomitable theological puzzle about Jesus' death. We have to explain theodicy: "Why does God allow evil to be rampant?" We cannot easily understand Jesus' tragic death simply in the name of love of God.[19] How can

others and also when they repent to God, for example at baptism in the gospel narratives. John the Baptist baptized people for the forgiveness of sins.

19. Here I use the term God's justice concerning theodicy. Otherwise, I know the satisfaction theory of atonement explains the need of Jesus' death which is a price of God's

we say that God is just or right by allowing for such a horrible torture on the cross? Where is God in this tragic event of Jesus' death? Regarding these questions, I have already touched on various traditional theological views of atonement focused on vicarious suffering of Jesus and God's redemptive co-suffering with Jesus and the oppressed. Jesus' cross is a place of violence and injustice that blocks God's justice. So from God's perspective, Jesus' cross is a tragic event and God has to judge those responsible for his death. At the cross we do not find God's justice, but God's judgment. It seems that God's justice is postponed and that evil wins. Even God seems to be silent or impotent at this very juncture of Jesus' death. Though we do not know God's mind at the moment of Jesus' suffering and death, one thing must be clear: Jesus' death does not show God's justice (that God is right or just). Rather, this death raises questions about God's justice. Is God just or right in the death of Jesus? The answer is no. However, from God's perspective, Jesus' death is more than a tragic death. Jesus is more than a victim because he risked his life for God and the world. The cross also shows Jesus' passion for God's rule in the here and now where there is a lack of God's mercy and love. The point is that we should not say that God is right in the death of Jesus, although Jesus' death shows his love and compassion for God and the world. But later in the gospel narrative we are told that God is right because he raises Jesus. At the cross God did not or could not do anything. That is a reality in the world even today where innocent people are hurt, captured, and killed in wars, for instance. Unless we are Deists who believe that God is not involved in daily matters of the world, or atheists who believe that there is no God, we have to grapple with the issue of theodicy, not to find the answer but to realize that there is no answer in the end and yet that we cannot give up pursuing God's justice.

On the flip side of God's justice (theodicy), we can think about Jesus' perspective and response to his tragic experience on the cross. How is God understood by him at the last moment when he felt abandoned by God and hopeless on the cross? What did he hope or demand when he lamented saying *eli eli lama sabachthani*? Jesus' feeling of hopelessness and powerlessness at that moment was so real that he must have believed that God had to do something for him even if such a help would not deliver him from the cross. But Jesus realizes that no one can save him from his cross

---

justice. But this theory is certainly not from the New Testament and puts God in bad light because God is viewed as an object of bargaining as in human business. Does God require the death of a sinless human to meet his highest moral justice, without which he cannot justify humanity? This idea is not in the New Testament.

now. So what would be his last thinking and hope about God? Readers can think from Jesus' perspective: "Now I am being killed by evil hands and out of weakness; no escape would be possible unless I recant. No divine help such as angels would come to save me. It is real that I am going to be executed." In this realization, Jesus must have hoped and prayed: "Even though you abandon me now, I have to believe that you will not abandon me completely because you are God and I believe I will live by your power. God, prove that you are just and right in the end and despite all this horrible death of your son. Show to the world that tortures and evil cannot win and that no single drop of blood of an innocent person may be shed on a cross anymore."

At the last moment of Jesus' death, his emotions must be complex. On the one hand, he feels he is so utterly forlorn that he laments about his unjust situation. On the other hand, he realizes that he cannot do anything at that moment and cannot expect God's help to save him. The only thing he can or must do is to hope for God's justice in two ways. First, his hope is about God's power that will make Jesus live even after his death. He believes that God will vindicate him and declare to the world that Jesus did not die in vain. Jesus showed the justice of God. Second, his hope is also about God's justice (that God is just or right). How will it be so? Because of his death, he hopes that the world may follow the way of God's rule and thus people may declare that God is right. They would say that Jesus' death is not in vain in the end. While he hopes and prays about this kind of a new world, Jesus, in view of the most difficult moment of his life, must have demanded or urged for God's justice after his death.

Summary

Jesus' crucifixion is a paradox of weakness that involves God's love, God's judgment, and God's justice (theodicy). On the one hand, Jesus was crucified out of weakness and by unjust political powers in Rome. So this aspect of Jesus' crucifixion calls for God's judgment on the evil power and people. On the other hand, Jesus was willing to die for God and the world, especially for the weak, in proclaiming the good news of God, not that of Rome. This aspect of Jesus' crucifixion embeds Jesus' love and solidarity with the weak and the oppressed. Nonetheless Jesus' crucifixion is not necessary for humanity's salvation. Ideally, the best scenario for Jesus was to deliver God's good news without being harmed or killed. But it did not happen because of those who blocked God's rule. As a result, an innocent life was sacrificed. Jesus' hopeful mission ended with weakness or ridicule, which raises questions about theodicy. Where is God in this horrible tragic death of Jesus? Is God right or just with this innocent death of Jesus? The answer is a resounding no; although, traditional atonement theories say yes. Theodicy is not resolved at the cross of Jesus because Jesus' death is tragic and done by Rome. Rather, Jesus' crucifixion is evidence of injustices. God's justice is partially resolved as Jesus is raised and vindicated by God. But it is yet to be shown completely in the world. Until then, the question of theodicy will remain, and we will continue to struggle to understand complexities of Jesus' crucifixion. There is no need of easy or hasty articulations about Jesus' crucifixion as understood in traditional atonement theories. Perhaps, one of the best ways to understand Jesus' life and death is, as Paul says, to "carry the marks of Jesus branded on my body" (Gal 6:17).

7

Conclusion

THUS WE HAVE COME full circle and are now addressing the same issue raised in the introduction: How can we approach the historical Jesus? My proposal was to interpret him from the perspective of the dispossessed—through the eyes of weakness. For this task, I also proposed an alternative understanding of weakness as a human condition and virtue. The fundamental assumption that this book holds and tests is that weakness is a lens through which Jesus sees God, the world, and humanity. Jesus lived through weakness and advocated for the weak. In the end he was crucified because of it. Interestingly, Paul also has a similar view of weakness as Jesus. Like Jesus, he realizes that this world is weak not because of satanic powers as such, but because of "the crooked human heart."[1] Romans 1:18–22 clearly locates the problem in humanity's disobedience to God's will:

> For the wrath of God is revealed from heaven against all ungodliness and wickedness of those who by their wickedness suppress the truth. For what can be known about God is plain to them, because God has shown it to them. Ever since the creation of the world his eternal power and divine nature, invisible though they are, have been understood and seen through the things he has made. So they are without excuse; for though they knew God, they did not honor him as God or give thanks to him, but they became futile in their thinking, and their senseless minds were darkened. Claiming to be wise, they became fools.

---

1. Calvin Roetzel says: "It is not bad Torah that brings to sin and death . . . but rather the crooked human heart." See Roetzel, *Letters of Paul*, 116.

The human problem is that the strong seek their own wealth and power at the expense of the weak.[2] Both Jesus and Paul try to remedy this problem of no godly rule in the world, advocating for the weak, challenging the powerful people to be weak before God and other people, who are also the image of God, and to seek the way of God. Both of them emphasize human participation in God's rule. In the case of Jesus, we saw his message of *metanoia* (Mark 1:15). No change of a heart, no rule of God with a person and community. Likewise, Paul clearly says: "The righteous person shall *live by faith*" (Rom 1:17). For Paul, an acceptable person to God is not someone who has mere faith in Jesus but someone who lives by faith. That is, a righteous person should live faithfully in God and in view of Jesus' faithful life.[3] What is required to live a faithful life for God? Paul's answer is to "put to death the deeds of the body" (Rom 8:13) and to imitate Jesus (1 Cor 4:16; 11:1). As a result, God's righteousness, equivalent to Jesus' teaching about God's rule, may be manifested to all (Rom 3:21–22).[4] Otherwise, Paul does not say that God's righteousness would come merely through your faith in Jesus. There must be a faith that is lived according to God's righteousness. For that matter, one has to cut the foreskin of the heart (Jer 4:4), which is translated into Paul's word: "Real circumcision is a matter of the heart; it is spiritual and not literal" (Rom 2:29). Here Paul urges people to see and attend to the need of others. To have this kind of a faithful life, one must be "weak" before God, as Paul eloquently states:

---

2. Paul's view of this human problem is also found in chapter 60 of the *Tao Te Ching*: "Leading a large country is like cooking a small fish. *When the world is ruled according to the Way, demons will be powerless.* It is not that they lose their power but that their power will no longer harm people. As demons do not harm people, the wise do not harm people. When both refrain from harming each other, all benefits will spread evenly to all people." Laozi basically says that human problems can be solved by humans if they follow the Way—the way of flexibility and mercy toward others. Similarly, as for Paul, the theological problem lies in humans and can be solved by humans if they live according to God's law. The only way that we can win sin's power is putting to death the deeds of the body as we read from Rom 8:13: "For if you live according to the flesh, you will die; but if by the Spirit you put to death the deeds of the body, you will live." See also Kim, *Why Christians Need to Read the Tao Te Ching*, 146–47.

3. Jesus' faith is what Paul emphasizes in his gospel. Gal 2:20 is a good test case: "and it is no longer I who live, but it is Christ who lives in me. And the life I now live in the flesh I live *in the faithfulness of the Son of God*, who loved me and gave himself for me" (Gal 2:20). The italicized part is the Greek genitive case, which implies that it is Jesus' faith that is lived by Paul. See Kim, *Resurrecting Jesus*.

4. See Kim, *Theological Introduction to Paul's Letters*.

> My grace is sufficient for you, for power is made perfect in weakness. So, I will boast all the more gladly of my weaknesses, so that the power of Christ may dwell in me. Therefore I am content with weaknesses, insults, hardships, persecutions, and calamities for the sake of Christ; for whenever I am weak, then I am strong (2 Cor 12:9–10).

Accordingly, Paul suggests that people have to have an alternative view of weakness as virtue. Paul declares, "For God's foolishness is wiser than human wisdom, and God's weakness is stronger than human strength" (1 Cor 1:25). Obviously, Paul means not that God is weak and foolish in common literal sense, but that people think God is foolish and weak because God does not subscribe to the dominant wisdom and culture, in which the strong and the rich are served at the sacrifice of the weak. Christ crucified is "a stumbling block to Jews and foolishness to Gentiles" (1 Cor 1:23). Rather, God takes the side of the weak and the foolish in society. That is the alternative, counter-cultural wisdom for which Jesus fought. Certainly, Jesus took the side of the weak, and the result was his crucifixion, as we saw in the previous chapter. Whereas Caesar says that wealth and social status is power, Paul declares that God's impartial love is power and that God chose the weak in the world. In 1 Cor 1:26–30, Paul vehemently defends such a love of God for the weak in the Corinthian church:

> Consider your own call, brothers and sisters: not many of you were wise by human standards, not many were powerful, not many were of noble birth. But God chose what is foolish in the world to shame the wise; God chose what is weak in the world to shame the strong; God chose what is low and despised in the world, things that are not, to reduce to nothing things that are, so that no one might boast in the presence of God. He is the source of your life in Christ Jesus, who became for us wisdom from God, and righteousness and sanctification and redemption, in order that, as it is written, "Let the one who boasts, boast in the Lord."

Laozi's *Tao Te Ching* and Weakness[5]

Though Laozi lived long before Jesus or Paul, his teaching on wisdom has a lot in common. Laozi is believed to have written the *Tao Te Ching* (the Book of the Way and Virtue). Among others, his view of weakness as virtue is outstanding. In his work, water is a symbol (metaphor) of both weakness and

5. See Kim, *Why Christians Need to Read the Tao Te Ching*, 14–191.

strength, on which he depends to explore an alternative wisdom. Chapter 8 of the *Tao Te Ching* is devoted to this topic of water's importance in human wisdom. The following is my translation of chapter 8 of the *Tao Te Ching*:

Chapter 8 of the *Tao Te Ching*

> Water is the best thing in the world.
> It benefits all things without competing with them.
> It flows to lower places that people do not want to go.
> Therefore it is closest to the Way.
> Look for lowly places.
> Look into the depth of all things.
> Treat others with mercy.
> Speak trusting words.
> Do right things when governing.
> Act mercifully and timely.
> Do not compete with others and there will be no fault with you.

Water does not fight others, but benefits all on earth by flowing everywhere. It does so by lowering itself. Like water, humans are asked to be humble and impartial to others. "Treat others with mercy" sounds like Jesus' teaching:

> You have heard that it was said, "You shall love your neighbor and hate your enemy." But I say to you, Love your enemies and pray for those who persecute you, so that you may be children of your Father in heaven; for he makes his sun rise on the evil and on the good, and sends rain on the righteous and on the unrighteous. For if you love those who love you, what reward do you have? Do not even the tax collectors do the same? And if you greet only your brothers and sisters, what more are you doing than others? Do not even the Gentiles do the same? Be perfect, therefore, as your heavenly Father is perfect. (Matt 5:43–48)

In Matt 12:7, Jesus also quotes from Hosea 6:6: "I desire mercy and not sacrifice." What is lacking in Jesus' time is mercy toward other people. Laozi's point is that people should not discriminate others based on any identity marker. In addition to Chapter 8, water as a symbol of weakness and strength is also found in chapters 34, 36, and 78. It is worth reading these chapters too.

Chapter 34 of the *Tao Te Ching*

> The great way of life is like a river
> of which its overflowing water goes to the left and right.
> All things depend on it for life, and it does not turn away from them.
> The Way accomplishes its work, but does not claim credit for it.
> It provides for and nourishes all things,
> but does not claim to be master over them.
> It does not seek its own will, and is considered small.
> All things come to it, but it does not control them.
> It never claims greatness, and therefore it is great.

Chapter 34 continues the theme of chapter 8 that we already saw above. In doing so, it gives us an image of a river with overflowing water. Laozi's point is that the work of water in the river is impartial, benefiting both the left and right sides of the river. Otherwise, river or water does not seek its own will. That is what the Way looks like.

Chapter 36 of the *Tao Te Ching*

> If you want to contract something, you must first stretch it.
> If you want to weaken something, you must first make it strong.
> If you want to tear down something, you must first raise it up.
> If you want to take something, you must first give it.
> This is called subtle illumination.
> What is soft and weak can overcome what is hard and strong.
> As fish should not leave water, sharp weapons of the state should not be shown to the people.

Laozi here talks about paradoxical truths that we observe and experience in our lives. He says that "what is soft and weak can overcome what is hard and strong." The soft and weak refers to water. If one has a mind of water, he or she is a strong person. Like water, one needs a mind of weakness or softness that does not hold on to particular things with closed mindset. There are numerous repetitions about this importance of a soft mind: empty mind (chapter 3–5, 11, 16, 22), soft mind (chapter 3–4, 10, 36, 43, 52, 55–56, 58, 76, 78), and weak mind (chapter 29, 36, 55, 76, 78). Indeed, this is the essence of Laozi's teaching in the *Tao Te Ching*.

Chapter 78 of the *Tao Te Ching*

> Nothing in the world is softer and weaker than water.
> Yet nothing is better for hitting hard and strong things.
> There is no substitute for it.
> The weak overcomes the strong; the soft overcomes the hard.
> All in the world know this, but no one puts it into practice.
> Therefore the wise say whoever suffers disgrace for the country is the owner of the country; whoever bears the misfortunes of the country is the lord of the world.
> True words seem paradoxical.

This chapter also echoes the chapters 8, 34, and 36 concerning the theme of water. The weak overcomes the strong; the soft overcomes the hard. The weak are those who suffer with other people; therefore, they are true leaders of the country.

In sum, water is easily found on earth and we cannot live without it. It is one of the softest or weakest things in the world. Paradoxically, however, because it is weak, it becomes strong. This is what Paul expressed in his faith about God: "My grace is sufficient for you, for power is made perfect in weakness. . . . For whenever I am weak, then I am strong" (2 Cor 12:9–10).

So Laozi teaches in chapter 33 that one should be strong by keeping softness (or weakness). He is more specific about who is a soft, strong person: "Those who conquer others are forceful. Those who conquer themselves are strong" (chapter 33 of the *Tao Te Ching*). People in Jesus' time or in Laozi's time seek their own greatness by competing and conquering others. For Jesus, a true person has to seek God's rule by changing their mind (*metanoia*), and for Laozi, a strong person is able to check his or her ambition. Laozi's teaching of "conquering of the self" is not comparable to the Stoics' teaching of self-control, which is more about inner control. Laozi's concern is not the loss of inner peace, but about the loss of justice and equality.

Weakness as a New Paradigm for Humanity

Whether in Laozi's time, in Jesus' time, or today, there is a common culture that seeks greatness or strength by sacrificing others. This is a binary logic that people think their success is because of others' failure. But both the "strong" and the "weak" can prosper together if there is a common ground of weakness, based on human vulnerability and solidarity. When one part in the body suffers, all suffer together. Through this lens of weakness, we can see holy faces in others.

In fact, strength is already within us. But we are slow to recognize it or completely ignore it. While some people believe that strength comes from heaven, others seek it from knowledge or social status. Each person is already born and equipped with such a gift of strength, which must be seen through the image of God. But this strength in each person is not automatically released because there is a way to unlock it. First, we should recognize that everyone is equipped with strength, being potentially good and beautiful. So we should and can be confident about that image of God within us. No one can say to others that "you are bad forever." With that judgment he or she will be judged. Second, we also should know that strength is not always or necessarily on the opposite side of weakness. Rather, strength can come from a "weakness experience" in our lives because we can learn from it. Strength also can come through sharing a common "brokenness" in our lives, which means a sense of co-suffering with others. For this matter, I am reminded by Laozi's famous word in the *Tao Te Ching* chapter 13, which emphasizes common suffering and solidarity, so to speak:

> Take both honor and disgrace as a pleasant surprise.
> Regard trouble and suffering as precious as your body.
> What does "taking disgrace and honor as a pleasant surprise" mean?
> It means you have to be humble.
> If things are going well, you are surprised with thanks.
> Even if things are not going well,
> you are surprised because you can learn from failure.
> What does "regarding trouble and suffering as precious as your body" mean?
> It means we suffer because we are a body.
> How can I suffer if I don't have a body?
> If you regard the world as precious as your body,
> you are entrusted to work for the world.
> If you love the world as your body,
> you can take care of the world.

Third, we also should know that nothing can separate us from the love of God, as Paul comforts his readers in Romans: "For I am convinced that neither death, nor life, nor angels, nor rulers, nor things present, nor things to come, nor powers, nor height, nor depth, nor anything else in all creation, will be able to separate us from the love of God in Christ Jesus our Lord" (Rom 8:38–39). This love of God is confirmed through Jesus' life and death as Paul says "the love of God" is manifested "in Christ Jesus our Lord." Earlier, Paul also said about Jesus' love: "Who will separate us from the love of Christ? Will hardship, or distress, or persecution, or famine, or nakedness, or peril, or sword?" (Rom 8:35). Love of God wins!

Excursus: Reading Biblical Characters through the Eyes of Weakness

We can reinterpret familiar biblical characters through the eyes of weakness, as we have explored in the case of the historical Jesus. For that purpose we will briefly look into their personal and communal environment concerning weakness and see how they respond to what they experience, positively or negatively. In this study we limit ourselves to the following characters in the Hebrew Bible (because we dealt with Jesus and Paul): (1) Abraham, (2) Sarah and Hagar, (3) Esau and Jacob, (4) Joseph, (5) Naomi and Ruth, (6) Hannah, (7) Elijah, and (8) Job. With the special reading lens of weakness explored in this book, the familiar stories about these characters will be better or clearer understood in terms of their character or ethics that involves an understanding of weakness and strength.

(1) Abraham

Abraham is the most important character in the Hebrew Bible since he is the beginning of the covenant made between God and Israel. Indeed, he becomes a model of faith by Paul in his letters (Romans and Galatians). In Genesis 12, Abraham is called out of nowhere and nobody; he is weak and old. His hometown is remote in Ur of Chaldea. His ancestors were meager and involved in idol worship. Abraham cannot be hopeful of his future. He cannot dream of it by himself. He does not have his posterity either. He is an archetype of a miserable person. He left his hometown in Ur and settled in Haran, which is still hard place to live. All this describes his social human condition that is so weak that he cannot hope for any good thing. All of sudden, as far as we know from Genesis, we have to say God's call is sudden. Abraham is called perhaps because he is ready for God's call. But we do not know. The point is that he is called by God and is given a new mission that he has to leave for the unknown place of hope. Abraham listens to God and trusts him as he moves forward with new hope. But in fact, Abraham's faith is not always consistently strong. At one point, his sense of justice for the people in community is so strong that he argues with God, demanding God's justice for the people in Sodom and Gomorrah. But at other points, like when God asks for the sacrifice of his son Isaac, Abraham is timid or passive about his attitude toward God. If he were caring father, he had to ask God: "What is the purpose of asking me to do this?" But in Genesis 21 readers are not told anything about Abraham's justice voice. He even lied to his son and did not tell him about what he was going to do. That is a horrible father. He does not care about his son. Where is his fatherhood? Where is his justice voice as he raised issues in Sodom and Gomorrah? Is his son less than people in Sodom and Gomorrah? He is so weak that he falls in fear. Perhaps this father has now blinded faith that cannot discern the will of God. Even if God asks such a nonsensical thing, he had to engage with God and had to say that it is not good. Blind faith is dangerous in that Isaac would have been sacrificed if not for the sudden call from heaven. Abraham followed the order with blind timid faith without engaging with God. Perhaps from the beginning God did not want Abraham to kill his son and offer him as a sacrifice, but only wanted to test him whether he had a faith of discernment or engagement.

What we can learn from Abraham's long journey of faith is this: He was weak *and* strong. He never gained faith once and for all. He was weak and called by God; he was strong enough. Nevertheless, he was so weak in his faith that he moved away from earlier strength. His life is made up of ups and downs, turns and twists. That is why I like Abraham. If he was perfect, I would not be able to imitate him and he would not be a model of faith. The important thing is to live a life of faith in the long run. Abraham's weakness became his strength when he was called by God. His hope or strength was not maintained well as he moved along with his journey. At the end of his journey, he was given a small lot as a burial place. That is not the end of glory. That is the reality we can follow. A great person of faith, in the end, is buried in small lot of land. But his faith life is remembered in both good and bad ways.

(2) Sarah and Hagar

Both Sarah and Hagar are women who are with Abraham. Sarah is the wife of Abraham and they did not have child. Hagar is a slave woman who bore a son to him. Sarah, as both a woman and a wife, was in a miserable situation because she was barren. She asked Abraham to sleep with Hagar so that they could continue with the journey of faith enacted by God. In this act of Sarah, her weakness is translated into an impatient improper technique that uses Hagar. This is the wrong exit for Sarah and she should not have asked. The result is so bitter that Sarah is involved in envying Hagar's childbearing and her son Ishmael. In the end Hagar is no more than the object of sex and abused by Sarah, who asks her husband to expel Hagar and her son together. Abraham, again with blind faith to God, listens to Sarah and evicts them into the wilderness. Sarah's tears in weakness turned to tears of jealousy and anger. Hagar and her innocent son Ishmael shed tears of victims. Whose tears should we embrace? As Hagar and Ishmael are taken care of in the wilderness, we should remember tears of these persons in the wilderness.

(3) Esau and Jacob

Jacob is the younger brother of Esau; and both of them are sons of Isaac. Jacob and Esau are very different in both their character and behavior. Where Esau is masculine in style and enjoys hunting—making him a favorite of Isaac—his brother, Jacob is feminine and womanish and enjoys cooking; so he is loved by his mother, Rebekah (Gen 25:27). As the story goes, Jacob sells the lentil stew he made to Esau in exchange for his birth right. Eventually, Jacob with the help of his mother deceives Isaac into blessing him instead of his brother Esau. This part of story shows that Jacob is morally deficient. He is wrong in this matter; he is not a model of faith. Esau was angry at this deception and threatened to kill his brother. That is at least the understandable voice of justice. So Jacob ran away to Lavan's house, who is his mother's rich uncle. For some reason, he wants to return home, but was not sure how Esau would respond to his homecoming. He struggles and prays a lot at Jabbok where he encounters deity and his name is changed to Israel. This new name suggests that he is reborn. But we are not told how he changed himself. I believe this is the time he became strong somehow. Until this time, he was busy deceiving others and making himself look great. Now he fights against himself and with God. After this event, perhaps he thought that was ready to meet Esau again. Unlike his sudden departure from his home, now there is no such a mode of haste with Jacob, and he and his wives and children slowly approach Esau and bow down to find favor. Bowing down and presenting valuable gifts to him are a sure sign that Jacob honors his brother. However, Jacob never uttered sure words of repentance about his stealing of the birthright from his brother Esau. Jacob seems to regret his rash action of stealing his brother's birthright. In a way, when Jacob was giving up a lot of his properties and presenting them to his brother, along with his new name, it seems that he became morally and spiritually strong. Now let us look at Esau. Readers are very surprised by his response to Jacob. He used to carry the image of a strong warrior and was very vocal about justice. Seeing Jacob, however, Esau ran to his brother and kissed him. This scene reminds us the parable of the Father and Two Sons in Luke 15:11–32 where the father accepts the younger son unconditionally. Readers are not told what happened to Esau to cause him to change his mind to accept and welcome his brother without vengeance. He could have done damage to his brother. But he was at least generous at this time. In a way, Esau's action resembles the typical mother's. Here we no longer see Esau as the masculine hunter-father figure in a traditional family. In a way, it seems that he becomes "truly" strong both morally and spiritually, through his mercy toward Jacob. Mercy can make a person stronger. This story does not tell us whether they truly reconciled because reconciliation needs time and further action. But overall, this story of Jacob and Esau tells the readers about what makes them strong and how they are transformed from weakness to strength. The negative portrayal of Esau in the overall story is because of the narrator (or the final editor of the Torah) of the story.

(4) Joseph

I am bothered by the sermon that teaches about Joseph's ambitious dream to be great. Many love this story of Joseph's dream as a model to follow. Typically, Joseph's success story is explained like this: if anyone has a great dream and endures to achieve it through faith, the dream comes true. I think the logic itself makes sense as we see in typical moral teaching where children are taught that they aim high and make efforts under any harsh environment. But from this book's lens of weakness, Joseph's story can be read very differently. First, Joseph's dream is so naive and shallow, focusing on himself (self-centered naive ambition). Readers are not told about the specific ethical or communal value-driven contents of his dream. His whole dream is childish, void of any good contents in terms of moral or communal value. In his dream, Joseph uses his parents and brothers to satisfy his goal. That is a model of the dictator. His dream is not only naive but ethically blinded. What good comes out of this dream? In the text, we know that Joseph is favored by Jacob. Joseph may have thought of himself as a "special" son, distinguished from his other brothers. Jacob's favoritism to Joseph seems to ruin Joseph's moral character from early on his life. Because of his father's blinded favor to him, Joseph grew with self-centered ambition. His morality is weak. As the story goes, readers are told that Joseph is sold by his brothers to the Midianite traders who again sold to Potiphar, an officer of Pharaoh. Joseph became weak in terms of his living condition. He must have been so confused about his earlier dream focused on the self. Living as an alien and slave in Egypt, Joseph somehow has to come up with new identity, different from his early naive personhood. He dealt with so many issues, from personal to national. Later, by a good chance in his difficult life in Egypt, he received an opportunity to interpret the king's dream and became a phenomenal successful figure there. Usually readers connect Joseph's early dream with this later success in Egypt. But I cannot read that way as I said earlier. My thesis is that while his early dream is just shallow and naive lacking good moral character, his later success reflects his tested time of hardships where his strength is shattered. I believe that he may have thought that his early childhood dream was ill-based. He could be a great person not because of his "aimless" dream to be great at his childhood, but because of his endurance and transformative experience in a foreign land. Only then success came upon him; otherwise, he did not seek to be a great person while living in so harsh a living condition.

In the end, without knowing, Joseph became strong, morally and spiritually, not because of his success but because of his long life journey of odyssey. In my imagination, Joseph may have regretted about his early naive dream that led to his long ordeal. He bothered his brothers, without which he would not have been sold to slavery. I believe Joseph at his last days in his life had mixed feelings about his life.

(5) Naomi and Ruth

Unlike Sarah and Hagar, Naomi and Ruth journey together for the common purpose of surviving and prospering in the midst of family crisis and economic hardships in a foreign land. Naomi, all of sudden, is bereaved of all male members in the family: her husband and all of her sons. Without males in the family, she cannot continue to live. In a most miserable situation, she becomes most weak personally and economically. So she decides to return to her homeland by herself because that is only option that she can make for herself and her daughters-in-law. As the story of Ruth goes, Ruth wants to go with her mother-in-law no matter what, whereas Orpah wants to stay in her homeland, which is exactly what her mother-in-law wants. So Orpah is obedient to her mother-in-law and also is loyal to her homeland by staying there. Orpah is a good woman who is sensible and realistic. Nothing bad is connoted about her in the text. She made her best choice, which is good for her. No one can speak against Orpah, whose responsibility is to live well going through kinds of weakness experience in her homeland. Without knowing how she goes through her life of ups and downs, no one can judge about her. But Ruth, from her own choice, decides to walk with Naomi and moves to Israel, which is a foreign land to her. Similar to Orpah, no one can judge Ruth because she left her homeland. She decided her own fate with hopes that she could live better. Naomi and Ruth, two of the most marginal women in this time, are faced with so many difficulties because they were women and without economic resources such as land. In this dire situation, Naomi devises a plan for success and survival with their bonded relationships: to earn favor from Boaz, kindred of Naomi. In a strict sense, what is happening in the story is sex-mediated business, which is to get married to a powerful male such as Boaz. The plan works out well. Some say it is divine help, but others say it is not so good to use sex as a means to achieve their goal of survival and prosperity. Interpreters are left with room to play with this sex-driven act in the field. On the one hand, both Naomi and Ruth are "realistic" characters of marginalized women who do not give up on their journey together and pursue their dream aggressively. In a way, they are smart enough to know where they go to find helper and to make success. On the other hand, modern interpreters with moral sensibility to women's relationships are not happy about this sex-driven technique for success. In this view, Naomi manipulates her daughter-in-law for her dream. Ruth is also aggressive to the same degree toward their common goal of a life: survival and prosperity. In the end, what they did with a means of sex is not desirable, because the good purpose cannot justify bad means. However, Ruth is a realistically beautiful story in which two "weak" women walk together, through ups and downs. They are not perfect models of faith, and yet they are good models of faith in certain ways.

(6) Hannah[6]

Hannah is another character in the Hebrew Bible who is one of the most marginalized women of her time. She was barren and treated poorly by the

---

6. For more about Hannah's transformative experience, see Kim, *Transformative Reading of the Bible*, 38–47.

other wife of her husband Elkanah. She was weak because of her barrenness and went to the Temple to pray. During the process of dealing with her weakness and social stigma, she is transformed into a person of communal faith and she swears to give her son back to God, dedicating him for the Temple and community. In this regard, she becomes a model of public faith beyond her personal one because she is more concerned with well being of the whole society. Hannah's weakness and tears turned into tears of joy and thanksgiving, not only because she is given Samuel but because she dedicates him back to God and the community. Hannah does not ask God to punish Peninnah who troubles her due to her barrenness, nor does she use Samuel to exact revenge on her. As she was weak before bearing Samuel, she chose to become weak once again by emptying her mind. As a result, she becomes strong! She shows the teaching that love wins.[7]

(7) Elijah

Elijah is one of the great prophets. He is an icon of power and prophecy and defeats the prophets of Baal. Most of the time, he shows strength; but he also becomes weak and trembling when Jezebel seeks to kill him because of his killing of Baal prophets. Elijah utters cries of hopelessness: "I have had enough, Lord; take my life. I am no better than my ancestors." Elijah is filled with real fear and he runs for his life. Where is his faith and courage that he made great works for God? Is this the picture of a great spiritual leader? As we saw with Abraham's realistic faith, even the great prophet Elijah had fear. But his fear is real. Indeed, he is a mere man, not an angel or god. His joy, energy, and passion for God on the mount of Carmel melted out just like snow under the sun. He is drained out and completely burned out. Nothing is left on him other than the desire to give up. Instead, Jezebel's threat filled him. Elijah was strong and weak. When a person is situated in this dire moment when nothing he or she can do other than the desire to give up, this is the moment of lament, of crying for God's justice and power. In Elijah's story the angel appears and provides for Elijah's needs. In a very dire moment like this, there must be an aid from outside of him. He cannot

---

7. In *A Transformative Reading of the Bible*, I argued that the proposed model of holistic human transformation, which is found in Hannah's story, is better than usual liberation models in that transformation means a change of one party only. I say the liberation model is run with the logic of "either/or." As we see in Hannah's story, she does not aim to defeat her enemy to make success. But she becomes a greater person than before because she embraces the whole community in the name of mercy and love. Samuel is supposed to do great work on behalf of his mother.

deal with everything by himself. Although he did a marvellous job on the mount of Carmel, those acts were God's, not his own. Often leaders forget this. When things go rough, they easily forget about God's grace or their identity in it. God wants him to go back on his journey. God's message is: "Hang in there; I will provide for you. You can give up on yourself. But don't give up on me." Elijah needs God's power once again. Elijah's strength cannot come from his success but from God. When faith fades and fear engulfs, we have to know this: "Nothing can separate us from the love of God" (Rom 8:28).

(8) Job

Job is a difficult story that we have to engage. It forces us to ask questions of theodicy (justice of God). Where is God when bad things happen to good people? Those who seek answers to these will be disappointed because the book of Job does not provide any of those. As we saw in the case of Jesus' crucifixion, one common issue is why a good person has to suffer. But there are differences between Jesus' crucifixion and Job's misery. Jesus' crucifixion may be expected in some way because he was involved in proclaiming the good news of God, which is against the good news of Rome. In some sense, Jesus was willing to die for God's rule and good news though his death was not necessary. For Job, however, his loss of everything—properties and children was sudden and for no apparent reason. The text says Job is a righteous person and lived a good life of faith. But all of sudden, he loses everything and his body is useless, being soaked with skin disease. He falls into deep ditches of despair that he cannot understand or explain. Even his wife asks him to die after cursing the God he trusts. He is in total despair. Job's friends do not understand him, asking him to repent of his sins so that God will restore him. Job knows that he does not deserve such a cruelly horrendous suffering and the loss of everything. He confronts a cruel unjust God honestly and laments about being born on earth. Virtually the best option for him is to end his life as soon as possible. Who can say suffering is valuable? Who can ask Job to repent? The God that he confronts is silent while his friends are talkative in giving definitive answers to Job. Toward the end of the book, God appears to Job and lets his mouth shut. Appearing in the storm-wind, God reminds Job of his mortality and the weakness embedded in humanity. God's question to Job is so real and right that no humans can answer: "Where were you when I laid the foundation of the earth?" (Job 38:4). The idea or answer behind this cruel question goes like this: "Job, you are unable to know why you suffer. You are mortal. Stay where you are. I will be with you when you go through a long deep dark tunnel." In the end, Job is not assured about his salvation other than God's being with him. We realize that Job is not the book of comfort or hope for the weak. We are constantly reminded that there is no sure answer about everything. We as readers ask what drives Job's faith. What is the basis of his faith? Can a person still trust God even when there is nothing hopeful within his or her reach? Ultimately, faith does not have to do with us or with what is happening now. Even though we do not understand why we suffer, we cannot give up our lives because we are not given sure answers yet. Until we face God, we have to live in faith and for faith.

Bibliography

Algra, Keimpe. "Stoic Theology." In *The Cambridge Companion to the Stoics*, edited by Brad Inwood, 153–78. Cambridge: Cambridge University Press, 2003.
Allison, Jr., Dale. *Constructing Jesus: Memory, Imagination, and History*. Grand Rapids: Baker, 2010.
———. *The Historical Christ and the Theological Jesus*. Grand Rapids: Eerdmans, 2009.
———. *Jesus of Nazareth: Millenarian Prophet*. Minneapolis: Fortress, 1998.
———. *Resurrecting Jesus: The Earliest Christian Tradition and Its Interpreters*. New York: T. & T. Clark, 2005.
Aristotle. *De Poetica*. Translated by St. Halliwell. Cambridge, MA: Harvard University Press, 1995.
———. *Nicomachean Ethics*. Translated by H. Rackham. Cambridge, MA: Harvard University Press, 1975.
Aslan, Reza. *Zealot: The Life and Times of Jesus of Nazareth*. New York: Random, 2013.
Aulen, Gustav. *Christus Victor. An Historical Study of the Three Main Types of the Idea of the Atonement*. New York: Macmillan, 1969.
Baillie, D. M. *God Was in Christ: An Essay on Incarnation and Atonement*. New York: Scribner, 1948.
Banks, Robert. *Jesus and the Law in the Synoptic Tradition*. Cambridge: Cambridge University Press, 1975.
Barnett, Paul. *The Message of 2 Corinthians*. Downers Grove, IL: InterVarsity, 1988.
Barrett, C. K. *Jesus and the Gospel Tradition*. Philadelphia, PA: Fortress, 1968,
Bauckham, Richard. *Jesus and the God of Israel: God Crucified and Other Studies on the New Testament's Christology of Divine Identity*. Grand Rapids: Eerdmans, 2008.
———. *The Theology of Jürgen Moltmann*. Edinburgh: T. & T. Clark, 1995.
Becker, Joachim. *Messianic Expectation in the Old Testament*. Philadelphia, PA: Fortress, 1980.
Beilby, James, and Paul Rhodes Eddy, eds. *The Historical Jesus: Five Views*. Downers Grove, IL: Intervarsity, 2009.
Binet-Sanglé, C. *La Folie de Jésus*. Paris: A. Maloine, 1908.
Borg, Marcus J. *Conflict, Holiness, and Politics in the Teaching of Jesus*. New York: Mellen, 1984.
———. *The Heart of Christianity: Rediscovering a Life of Faith*. New York: HarperOne, 2004.
———. *Jesus: A New Vision*. New York: Harper Collins, 1987.
———. *Jesus in Contemporary Scholarship*. Harrisburg, PA: Trinity, 1994.

———. *Jesus: Uncovering the Life, Teachings, and Relevance of a Religious Revolutionary.* New York: Harper Collins, 2006.

———. *Meeting Jesus Again for the First Time: The Historical Jesus and the Heart of Contemporary Faith.* New York: HarperSanFrancisco, 1994.

Borg, Marcus, and N. T. Wright. *The Meaning of Jesus: Two Visions.* New York: Harper SanFrancisco, 1999.

Brennan, Tad. "Stoic Moral Psychology." In *The Cambridge Companion to the Stoics*, edited by Brad Inwood, 257–94. Cambridge: Cambridge University Press, 2003.

———. *The Stoic Life.* Oxford: Clarendon, 2005.

Brickhouse, Thomas, and Nicholas Smith. *Socratic Moral Psychology.* New York: Cambridge University Press, 2012.

Brown, Raymond E. *The Death of the Messiah: From Gethsemane to the Grave: A Commentary on the Passion Narratives in the Four Gospels.* 2 vols. Mahwah, NJ: Paulist, 1994.

Buttrick, David. *Speaking Parables: A Homiletic Guide.* Louisville, KY: Westminster John Knox, 2000.

Calvin, John. *Institutes of the Christian Religion.* 2 vols. Edited by John T. McNeill. Translated by Ford L. Battles. Louisville, KY: Westminster John Knox, 1960.

Capps, Donald. *Jesus the Village Psychiatrist.* Louisville, KY: Westminster John Knox, 2008.

Cartlidge, David and David Dungan, eds. *Documents for the Study of the Gospels.* Philadelphia, PA: Fortress, 1980.

Casey, Maurice. *The Solution to the "Son of Man" Problem.* LNTS 343. London: T. & T. Clark, 2007.

Cassuto, Umberto. *The Documentary Hypothesis.* Jerusalem: Shalem, 2006.

Chapman, David. *Ancient Jewish and Christian Perceptions of Crucifixion.* Tübingen: Mohr/Siebeck, 2008.

Chariton. *Chaireas and Callirhoe.* Translated by G. P. Goold. Cambridge, MA: Harvard University Press, 1995.

Charlesworth, James. *The Historical Jesus: The Essential Guide.* Nashville, TN: Abingdon, 2008.

Cicero. *De finibus.* Translated by H. Rackham. Cambridge, MA: Harvard University Press, 1914.

———. *Tusculanae Quaestiones.* Translated by Andrew Peabody. Boston, MA: Little, Brown, 1886.

Clarke, Sathianathan and Deenabandhu Manchala, eds. *Dalit Theology in the Twenty First Century: Discordant Voices, Discerning Pathways.* New York: Oxford University Press, 2010.

Collins, John. "A Messiah before Jesus?" In *Christian Beginnings and the Dead Scrolls*, edited by John Collins and Craig Evans, 15–35. Grand Rapids: Baker, 2006.

Cone, James. *A Black Theology of Liberation.* Mary Knoll, NY: Orbis, 2010.

Cooper, John. *Pursuits of Wisdom: Six Ways of Life in Ancient Philosophy from Socrates to Plotinus.* Princeton, NJ: Princeton University Press, 2012.

———. *Reason and Emotion.* Princeton, NJ: Princeton University Press, 1999.

Copeland, M. Shawn. *Enfleshing Freedom: Body, Race, and Being.* Minneapolis: Fortress, 2010.

Craddock, Fred. *Luke.* Louisville, KY: Westminster John Knox, 1990.

Crossan, John Dominic. *The Birth of Christianity.* New York, NY: Harper Collins, 1998.

———. *Excavating Jesus: Beneath the Stones, Behind the Texts.* New York: Harper Collins, 2001.

———. *In Parables. The Challenge of the Historical Jesus.* New York: Harper & Row, 1973.

———. *The Historical Jesus: The Life of a Mediterranean Jewish Peasant.* New York: Harper Collins, 1991.

———. *Jesus: A Radical Biography.* San Francisco, CA: HarperCollins, 1994.

Crossan, John, Luke Timothy Johnson, and Werner H. Kelber. *The Jesus Controversy: Perspectives in Conflict.* Harrisburg, PA: Trinity Press International, 1999.

Culbertson, Philip. "Changing Christian Images of the Pharisees." *Anglican Theological Review* 64.4 (1982) 539–61.

———. "The Pharisaic Jesus and His Parables." *Christian Century* (1985) 74–77.

Culpepper, R. Alan. "Contours of the Historical Jesus." In *The Quest for the Real Jesus*, edited by Jan Van der Watt, 67–85. Leiden: Brill, 2013.

Davies, Stevan. *Jesus the Healer: Possession, Trance, and the Origins of Christianity.* London: SCM, 1995.

Dawn, Marva. *Powers, Weakness, and the Tabernacling of God.* Grand Rapids: Eerdmans, 2001.

De Boer, Martinus. "Ten Thousand Talents: Matthew's Interpretation and Redaction of the Parable of the Unforgiving Servant (Matt 18:23–35)." *Catholic Biblical Quarterly* 50.2 (1988) 214–32.

De Loosten, G. L. *Jesus Christus vom Standpunkt des Psychiaters.* Bamberg: Handels-Druckerei, 1905.

Derrida, Jacques. *Of Grammatology.* Translated by Gayatri Spivak. Baltimore, MA: Johns Hopkins University Press, 1974.

Dio Chrysostom. *Discourses 31–36.* Translated by J. W. Cohoon. Cambridge, MA: Harvard University Press, 1940.

———. *Discourses 37–60.* Translated by H. Lamar Crosby. Cambridge, MA: Harvard University Press, 1946.

Diogenes Laërtius. *Lives of Eminent Philosophers.* Book 7. Translated by R. D. Hicks. Cambridge, MA: Harvard University Press, 1925.

Dunn, James D.G. *Jesus and the Spirit.* London: SCM, 1975.

Ehrman, Bart. *Jesus: Apocalyptic Prophet of the New Millennium.* New York: Oxford University Press, 1999.

Eve, Eric. *The Jewish Context of Jesus' Miracles.* JSNTSup 231. London: Sheffield, 2002.

Farley, Wendy. *Gathering Those Driven Away: A Theology of Incarnation.* Louisville, KY: Westminster John Knox, 2011.

Ferguson, Everett. *Backgrounds of Early Christianity.* Grand Rapids: Eerdmans, 2003.

Fitzmyer, Joseph A. *The Gospel According to Luke (X-XXIV)*, vol. 2. Garden City, NY: Doubleday, 1985.

France, R. T. *Jesus and the Old Testament: His Application of Old Testament Passages to Himself and His Mission.* Vancouver, BC: Regent College Publishing, 1998.

Fredriksen, Paula. *Jesus of Nazareth, King of the Jews: A Jewish Life and the Emergence of Christianity.* New York: Vintage, 1999.

Freyne, Sean. *Jesus, a Jewish Galilean: A New Reading of the Jesus Story.* New York: T. & T. Clark, 2004.

———. *The Jesus Movement and Its Expansion: Meaning and Mission.* Grand Rapids: Eerdmans, 2014.

Funk, Robert. *Honest to Jesus: Jesus for a New Millennium.* New York: HarperSanFrancisco, 1997.
Gaffin Jr., Richard. *Resurrection and Redemption: A Study in Paul's Soteriology.* Phillipsburg, NJ: Presbyterian & Reformed, 1987.
Glancy, J. A. "Boasting of Beatings (2 Corinthians 11:23–25)." *Journal of Biblical Literature* 123 (2004) 99–135.
Gorman, Michael. *The Death of the Messiah and the Birth of the New Covenant: A (Not So) New Model of the Atonement.* Eugene, OR: Cascade, 2014.
———. *Inhabiting the Cruciform God: Kenosis, Justification, and Theosis in Paul's Narrative Soteriology.* Grand Rapids: Eerdmans, 2009.
Gorman, Peter. *Pythagoras: A Life.* Boston, MA: Routledge, 1979.
Gowler, David B. *What Are They Saying About the Historical Jesus?* New York: Paulist, 2007.
Grabe, Petrus. *The Power of God in Paul's Letters.* Tübingen: Mohr/Siebeck, 2008.
Gudmundsdottir, Arnfridur. *Meeting God on the Cross: Christ, The Cross, and the Feminist Critique.* New York: Oxford University Press, 2011.
Guthrie, Kenneth. *The Pythagorean Sourcebook and Library: An Anthology of Ancient Writings Which Relate to Pythagoras and Pythagorean Philosophy.* Grand Rapids: Phanes, 1987.
Hanson, K. C. and Douglas E. Oakman. *Palestine in the Time of Jesus.* Minneapolis, MN: Fortress, 1998.
Hauerwas, Stanley, and Jean Vanier. *Living Gently in a Violent World: The Prophetic Witness of Weakness.* Downers Grove, IL: Intervarsity, 2008.
Herzog, William. *Parables as Subversive Speech: Jesus as Pedagogue of the Oppressed.* Louisville, KY: Westminster John Knox, 1994.
Hirsch, W. *Religion und Civilisation.* Munchen: Bonsels, 1910.
Horsley, Richard. *Archaeology, History, and Society in Galilee: The Social Context of Jesus and the Rabbis.* New York: T. & T. Clark, 1996.
———. *Bandits, Prophets, and Messiahs: Popular Movements in the Time of Jesus.* New York: T. & T. Clark, 1999.
———. *Galilee: History, Politics, People.* New York: T. & T. Clark, 1995.
———. *Hearing the Whole Story: The Politics of Plot in Mark's Gospel.* Louisville, KY: Westminster John Knox, 2001.
———. *Jesus and Empire: The Kingdom of God and the New World Disorder.* Minneapolis, MN: Fortress, 2002.
———. *Jesus and the Spiral of Violence: Popular Jewish Resistance in Roman Palestine.* New York: Harper, 1987.
———. *The Liberation of Christmas: The Infancy Narratives in Social Context.* New York: Crossroad, 1989.
———. *Sociology and the Jesus Movement.* New York: Crossroad, 1989.
———. *Whoever Hears You Hears Me: Prophets, Performance, and Tradition in Q.* New York: T. & T. Clark, 2000.
Howard, J. K. *Disease and Healing in the New Testament: An Analysis and Interpretation.* Lanham, MI: University Press of America, 2001.
Inwood, Brad. "Introduction: Stoicism, An Intellectual Odyssey." In *The Cambridge Companion to the Stoics*, edited by Brad Inwood, 1–6. Cambridge: Cambridge University Press, 2003.
Irwin, Terence. *Plato's Ethics.* New York, NY: Oxford University Press, 1995.

Johnson, Luke Timothy. *The Real Jesus: The Misguided Quest for the Historical Jesus and the Truth of the Traditional Gospels.* New York: HarperSanFrancisco, 1996.

Josephus. *Jewish Antiquities. Books 12–13.* Translated by Ralph Marcus. Cambridge, MA: Harvard University Press, 1943.

———. *Jewish Antiquities. Books 18–19.* Translated by Louis H. Feldman. Cambridge, MA: Harvard University Press, 1965.

Keck, Leander. *Who Is Jesus? History in Perfect Tense, Studies on Personalities of the New Testament.* Colombia, SC: University of South Carolina Press, 2000.

Kee, Howard. *What Can We Know About Jesus, Understanding Jesus Today.* Cambridge: Cambridge University Press, 1995.

Kim, Yung Suk. *1 and 2 Corinthians.* Minneapolis, MN: Fortress, 2013.

———. *Biblical Interpretation: Theory, Process, and Criteria.* Eugene, OR: Pickwick, 2013.

———. *Christ's Body in Corinth: The Politics of a Metaphor.* Minneapolis, MN: Fortress, 2008.

———. "*Lex Talionis* in Exod 21:22–25: Its Origin and Context." *Journal of Hebrew Scriptures* 6.3 (2006).

———. *Resurrecting Jesus: The Renewal of New Testament Theology.* Eugene, OR: Cascade, 2015.

———. *A Theological Introduction to Paul's Letters: Exploring a Threefold Theology of Paul.* Eugene, OR: Cascade, 2011.

———. *A Transformative Reading of the Bible.* Eugene, OR: Cascade, 2013.

———. *Truth, Testimony, and Transformation: Explorations of Holistic Human Transformation.* Eugene, OR: Cascade, 2013.

———. *Why Christians Need to Read the Tao Te Ching.* Charleston, SC: CreateSpace, 2014.

Kim, Yung Suk and Jin-Ho Kim, eds., *Reading Minjung Theology in the Twenty-first Century.* Eugene, OR: Pickwick, 2013.

Kolb, Robert, and Charles P. Arand. *The Genius of Luther's Theology: A Wittenberg Way of Thinking for the Contemporary Church.* Grand Rapids: Baker, 2008.

Levine, A. J. *Short Stories by Jesus: The Enigmatic Parables of a Controversial Rabbi.* San Francisco, CA: HarperOne, 2014.

Livy. *History of Rome. Books 1–2.* Translated by B. O. Foster. Cambridge, MA: Harvard University Press, 1919.

Lüdemann, Gerd. *The Great Deception: And What Jesus Really Said and Did.* Amherst, NY: Prometheus, 1999.

McGrath, Alistair. *Luther's Theology of the Cross: Martin Luther's Theological Breakthrough.* Oxford: Blackwell, 1985.

Meier, John P. *A Marginal Jew: Rethinking the Historical Jesus.* Vol. 1: The Roots of the Problem and the Person. New York: Doubleday, 1991.

———. *A Marginal Jew: Rethinking the Historical Jesus.* Vol 2: Mentor, Message, and Miracles. New York: Doubleday, 1994.

———. *A Marginal Jew: Rethinking the Historical Jesus.* Vol 3: Companions and Competitors. New York: Doubleday, 2001.

———. *A Marginal Jew: Rethinking the Historical Jesus.* Vol 4: Law and Love. New York: Doubleday, 2009.

Mercedes, Anna. *Power For: Feminism and Christ's Self-giving.* London: T. & T. Clark, 2011.

Meyers, Carol. *Discovering Eve: Ancient Israelite Women in Context.* New York: Oxford University Press, 1988.

Miller, Robert. ed. *The Apocalyptic Jesus: A Debate*. Santa Rosa, CA: Polebridge, 2001.

———. *The Jesus Seminar and Its Critics*. Santa Rosa, CA: Polebridge, 1999.

Moltmann, Jürgen. *Theology of Hope: On the Ground and the Implications of a Christian Eschatology*. Translated by James W. Leitch. Minneapolis, MN: Fortress, 1993.

Moxnes. Halvor. "Identity in Jesus' Galilee—From Ethnicity to Locative Intersectionality." *Biblical Interpretation* 18.4 (2010) 390–416.

Oakman, Douglas. *The Political Aims of Jesus*. Minneapolis, MN: Fortress, 2012.

O'Collins, Gerald. "Power Made Perfect in Weakness: 2 Cor. 12:9–10." *Catholic Biblical Quarterly* 33 (1971) 528–37.

O'Day, Gail. "John." In *The New Interpreter's Study Bible*, edited by Walter Harrelson, 1905–51. Nashville, TN: Abingdon, 2003.

Ortlund, Dane. "Power is Made Perfect in Weakness (2 Cor 12:9): A Biblical Theology of Strength through Weakness." *Presbyterion* 36.2 (2010) 86–108.

Patterson, Stephen. *The Gospel of Thomas and Jesus*. Sonoma, CA: Polebridge, 1994.

Peppard, Michael. *The Son of God in the Roman World: Divine Sonship in its Social and Political Context*. New York: Oxford University Press, 2011.

Philo. *De Abrahamo*. Translated by F. H. Colson. Cambridge, MA: Harvard University Press, 1935.

———. *De Fuga et Inventione*. Translated by F. H. Colson and G. H. Whitaker. Cambridge, MA: Harvard University Press, 1934.

———. *De Migratione Abrahami*. Translated by F. H. Colson and G. H. Whitaker. Cambridge, MA: Harvard University Press, 1932.

———. *De Opificio Mundi*. Translated by F. H. Colson and G. H. Whitaker. Online: http://www.earlyjewishwritings.com/text/philo/book1.html.

———. *De Specialibus Legibus*. Translated by F. H. Colson. Cambridge, MA: Harvard University Press, 1939.

———. *De Virtutibus*. Translated by F. H. Colson. Cambridge, MA: Harvard University Press, 1939.

———. *Legum Allegoriarum*. Translated by F. H. Colson and G. H. Whitaker. Online: http://www.earlyjewishwritings.com/text/philo/book4.html.

———. *Quaestiones et Solutiones in Genesim*. Translated by F. H. Colson and G. H. Whitaker. Online: http://www.earlyjewishwritings.com/text/philo/book41.html.

Plato. *Republic*. Books 1–5. Translated by Christopher Emlyn-Jones and William Preddy. Cambridge, MA: Harvard University Press, 2013.

Powell, Mark Allan. *Jesus as a Figure in History: How Modern Historians View the Man from Galilee*. Louisville, KY: Westminster John Knox, 2013.

Reid, Barbara. *Parables for Preachers*. Collegeville, MN: Liturgical, 1999.

Remus, Harold. *Jesus as Healer, Understanding Jesus Today*. Cambridge: Cambridge University Press, 1997.

Ridderbos, Herman. *Paul: an Outline of His Theology*. Grand Rapids: Eerdmans, 1975.

Roetzel, Calvin. "The Language of War (2 Cor. 10:1–6) and the Language of Weakness (2 Cor. 11:21b-13:10)." *Biblical Interpretation* 17 (2009) 77–99.

———. *The Letters of Paul*. Louisville, KY: Westminster John Knox, 2009.

Sanders, E. P. *Jesus and Judaism*. Philadelphia, PA: Fortress, 1985.

Schaberg, Jane. *The Illegitimacy of Jesus: A Feminist Theological Interpretation of the Infancy Narratives*. San Francisco, CA: Harper & Row, 1987.

Schlatter, Adolf. *The History of the Christ: The Foundations for New Testament Theology*. Grand Rapids: Baker, 1997.

———. *Paulus, der Bote Jesus: Eine Deutung seiner Briefe an die Korinther.* Stuttgart: Calwer, 1934.
———. *The Theology of the Apostles.* Grand Rapids: Baker, 1997.
Schweitzer, Albert. *The Psychiatric Study of Jesus: Exposition and Criticism.* San Francisco, CA: Beacon, 1950.
———. *The Quest of the Historical Jesus: A Critical Study of Its Progress from Reimarus to Wrede.* New York: Macmillan, 1961.
Scott, Brandon. *Hear Then the Parable.* Minneapolis, MN: Fortress, 1990.
———. "The King's Accounting: Matthew 18:23–34." *JBL* 104.3 (1985) 429–42.
———. *Re-Imagine the World: An Introduction to the Parables of Jesus.* Santa Rosa, CA: Polebridge, 2007.
Shaw, B. D. "Body/Power/Identity: Passions of the Martyrs." *Journal of Early Christian Studies* 4 (1996) 269–312.
Sobrino, Jon, SJ. *Jesus the Liberator.* Mary Knoll, NY: Orbis, 1994.
Stanley, Thomas. *Pythagoras: His Life and Teachings* Lake Worth, FL: Ibis, 2010.
Stein, Robert. *Jesus the Messiah: A Survey of the Life of Christ.* Downers Grove, IL: InterVarsity, 1996.
———. *The Method and Message of Jesus' Teachings.* Louisville: Westminster John Knox, 1994.
Stott, John. *The Cross of Christ.* Downers Grove, IL: InterVarsity, 2006.
Sumney, Jerry. "Paul's 'Weakness': An Integral Part of His Conception of Apostleship." *JSNT* 52 (1993) 71–91.
Tabor, James. "A Historical Look at the Birth of Jesus: Part 4." Personal Blog. Online: http://jamestabor.com/2012/12/26/a-historical-look-at-the-birth-of-jesus-part-4.
Tacitus. *Annals.* Books 13–16. Translated by John Jackson. Cambridge, MA: Harvard University Press, 1937.
Tomlin, Graham. *The Power of the Cross: Theology and the Death of Christ in Paul, Luther and Pascal.* Eugene, OR: Wipf and Stock, 2007.
Vermes, Geza. *Jesus the Jew.* London: Collins, 1973.
Wafawanaka, Robert. *Am I Still My Brother's Keeper? Biblical Perspectives on Poverty.* New York: University Press of America, 2012.
Webb, Elizabeth. "Power in Weakness: Feminist Reclamations of the Suffering of Christ." *Religious Studies Review* 38.4 (2012) 199–205.
Welborn, L. L. "The Runaway Paul." *Harvard Theological Review* 92 (1999) 115–63.
———. *Paul, the Fool of Christ: A Study of 1 Corinthians 1–4 in the Comic-Philosophic Tradition.* New York: T. & T. Clark, 2005.
———. "Paul and Pain: Paul's Emotional Therapy in 2 Corinthians 1:1–2:13; 7:5–16 in the Context of Ancient Psychagogic Literature." *New Testament Studies* 57 (2011) 547–70.
Wenham, David. *Christ and the Bible.* Downers Grove, IL: InterVarsity, 1972.
Wild, Robert. "The Encounter between Pharisaic and Christian Judaism: Some Early Gospel Evidence." *Novum Testamentum* 27.2 (1985) 105–24.
Worthington, Bruce. *Reading the Bible in an Age of Crisis: Political Exegesis for a New Day.* Minneapolis, MN: Fortress, 2015.
Wright, N. T. *Jesus and the Victory of God.* Minneapolis, MN: Fortress, 1997.

Subject Index

A
Abraham, 2, 126–28
Adam, 2, 8, 32, 35
agathos, 77
agency, 112
allegorical, 86
Amos, 39–41, 45
andreia (courage), 29, 45
anthropology, 36–37
apocalyptic: literature, 13; prophet, 7, 9–11, 13
Apollonius of Tyana, 27
Apostles' Creed, 2
Aristotle, 26–30
atonement theories, 109–11, 114, 118
Augustus, 47

B
Babylonian exile, 37, 56
Boer, Martinus, 83
Borg, Marcus, 13–16, 58n20, 98
boulesis (will), 30
brokenness, 17, 77, 125

C
Caesar, 25, 121
chara (joy), 30
Chariton, 25
Christology, 102, 108
Cicero, 30–31
circumcision, 41, 120
cognitive dissonance, 50, 99
consciousness, 15
conversion disorder, 97
Copeland, M. Shawn, 113
covenant, 38, 41, 43, 67
creation story, 2, 32–33, 35, 46
criterion of embarrassment, 11, 52
Crossan, John, 12, 52

D
Dalit theology, 11
Davies, Stevan, 13n30, 98
debt, 82–85
Deuteronomistic history, 38, 54
dignity, 24, 31, 34
dikaiosyne, 29, 45
discernment, 63, 95, 127
documentary hypothesis, 35n1
dualism, 27–29, 33–34, 111
dysfunctional family, 86, 89

E
economic justice, 76
ekdikeo, 90
ex astheneias, 3n2
Elijah, 126, 132–33
en christo, 49
enactment, 69
epithumia (desire), 30
Esau, 126, 128–29
Essenes, 43–44
eudamonia, 31
eulabeia (caution), 30
evil, 5–6, 12, 20–22, 32, 48, 50, 63, 74, 83, 91, 108–18, 122

exodus, 66–67
exorcism, 14, 97
Ezra, 37

F
faith, 3–4, 19, 22, 47–49, 61, 66, 90–91, 99–100, 104–5, 115, 120, 126–29, 131–34
family, 14, 45, 47, 51–52, 68, 75, 77, 84–89, 99, 129–30
Farley, Wendy, 113
favoritism, 88, 129
feminist theology, 108
forgiveness, 22, 64n25, 83–84, 89, 115
fornication, 51
Fourth Philosophy, 43
frailty, 6, 33, 36
Fredriksen, Paula, 9–10
full employment, 76
Funk, Robert, 12

G
gender, 26, 75
Gethsemane, 63, 107
Gnosticism, 28
good news of God, 4, 60, 69n1, 107, 111, 113–14, 117, 133
God's: area, 11; business, 5; foolishness, 6, 121; judgment, 9n18, 108–9, 114–17; power, 5–6, 21, 62, 99, 117; presence, 11, 30, 67; revelation, 4, 11; rule, 4–5, 10–11, 18–23, 44, 51, 60, 63, 65, 69–84, 88–105, 107–17, 125, 134; time, 10; weakness, 6, 45n16, 59, 121
grace, 18–9, 44, 94, 97, 104, 121, 124–25, 133
Gudmundsdottir, Arnfridur, 112

H
Hagar, 126–30
hallucination, 67n29, 99
Hannah, 37n3, 126, 131–32
Hauerwas, Stanley, 3n5
healing, 14, 55–61, 68, 70, 95–105

Hellenistic Judaism, 24, 27, 32–33
holiness, 14–15
holy death, 107, 109, 114–15
Holy Spirit, 51n13, 55–57
homonoia (concord), 31, 37
Horsley, Richard, 12
Hosea, 45, 69, 122
human condition, 1–3, 6, 16–17, 28, 84, 119, 126
human reason, 28
human transformation, 3, 12n24, 16, 37n3, 132n7
humanitarian laws, 38

I
imitation (mimesis), 29–30
incarnation, 27, 47–48, 110, 113
indignation, 53, 96
individual salvation, 12n24, 110–11
injustices, 17, 22, 31, 34, 90, 96, 112, 115, 118
innocent life, 118
Isaac, 2, 127

J
Jacob, 2, 126–30
Jairus, 104
Jeremiah, 40–41, 45, 92
Jerusalem, 15, 20, 38, 43, 49, 54–56, 65, 80, 108, 113
Jesus' death, 4–5, 21–23, 64, 106–18
Jesus' humanity, 7, 15, 49, 111
Jewish apocalypticism, 10
Jewish tradition, 11, 22, 32, 35, 43, 51, 58, 70, 95
John the Baptist, 10, 57, 60, 65
Jordan, 19, 60, 63, 65–66
Josephus, 20n44, 26, 42–43, 50

K
kenosis, 112
kyrios, 83

L
lament, 59, 63–64, 95, 118, 132–33
Last Supper, 62

Subject Index

law of the Spirit, 57
leaven, 73
liberation theology, 11
liberator, 6, 11–13
Logos, 32, 48, 57
lost sheep, 78–79

M

martyrdom theology, 4n8
Menenius, 25, 31n39
Mercedes, Anna, 111–12
messianic age, 10
metanoia, 10, 120, 124
minjung theology, 11
moderation (sophrosyne), 29, 45
Mosaic Law, 38
Moses, 14, 32, 38, 67, 90, 101

N

Naomi, 126, 130–31
Nazareth, 47, 49–52, 60, 64–65
Neo-Platonism, 3n3
Neopythagoreanism, 27
new creation, 49
new paradigm, 124
Noth, Martin, 38

O

Ortlund, Daniel, 7–8

P

pain (*lype*), 30
parakletos (Advocate), 57
paranoia, 98
paterfamilias, 87
pathos (feeling), 30
patron-client, 24–25, 76
Philo, 32–33
phobos (fear), 30
Pilate, 20, 106
Plato, 26–30
pleasure (hedone), 30
Polycarp, 4n8
post-Easter Christians, 13
poverty, 3, 52–53, 65
prayers, 59–64, 95

proclamation, 20, 99
prudence (*phronesis*), 29, 45
psychiatrist, 97–98
psychopathological disorder, 98
psychosomatic, 97
Pythagoras, 27–28

Q

Qumran, 43

R

reconciliation, 87–89, 129
redemptive suffering, 6, 109
reformer, 6, 10, 13, 15, 114
renewal, 12, 15, 38, 42, 67, 96, 99
repentance, 40, 78, 86–88, 128
restoration, 17, 44, 62, 88–89, 94, 103
resurrection of the dead, 2, 42
Rome's rule, 20–21, 50, 88, 106–9, 111, 114

S

sacrifice, 59, 61, 67, 69, 74, 111, 114, 119, 121–28
Sadducees, 2, 42, 44
Samaritan, 80–81, 87
salvific death, 110n7
Schweitzer, Albert, 66n29, 98–99, 114
self-control, 1, 30–32, 124
self-giving, 109, 111–14
Seneca, 30–31
Sepphoris, 50, 65
social activism, 70, 95–96, 105
social gospel, 11
Socrates, 1, 27–31
softness, 17, 123–24
solidarity, 3, 13, 20, 22, 68, 70, 79, 80, 91, 97, 105, 109, 113, 117, 125
Spirit-filled, 6, 13–14, 98
spirit-talk, 54–56
spiritual: battery, 60; birth, 57; body, 2; contact, 100
spirituality, 3, 40–41
splanchnizomai, 103
Stoicism, 24, 30, 33

Subject Index

strength, 1–7, 17, 22, 24, 36–37, 45–46, 59–60, 82, 108, 121–34
suffering love, 112
symbols, 54, 67

T
tekton, 47, 51–52, 58, 65
thanksgiving, 62, 67, 85, 95, 132
theodicy, 107, 115–18
Tiberius, 20
trauma, 97
tragic: death, 5, 110n7, 115–16, 118; event, 20, 112, 114–16
truth of God, 4, 23, 63, 111, 115

U
unmerciful servant, 82

V
vineyard, 39–40, 75–77
virtue, 1, 3, 6, 14, 17, 28–34, 45, 68–69, 96, 105, 119, 121

voluntary suffering, 107, 112, 115

W
water baptism, 54, 57, 60, 64
weakness: source of, 52; human, 8, 28–9, 37, 108; of Jesus, 5; vicarious, 7; of God, 5n10; moral, 7–8; lens of, 16–7, 70, 105, 125–26, 129; eyes of, 7, 16–19, 45, 59, 68–70, 73, 76, 78–80, 86–95, 107, 120, 127
Welborn, Larry, 19n42, 30
Western Jesus, 7–8, 11–12

Y
Yom Kippur, 40

Z
Zeno, 28, 30

www.ingramcontent.com/pod-product-compliance
Lightning Source LLC
Chambersburg PA
CBHW022125160426
43197CB00009B/1153